MEASURING THE SUCCESS OF YOUR WEBSITE

A CUSTOMER-CENTRIC APPROACH TO WEBSITE MANAGEMENT

DEDICATION

To the living memory of my father, Hayati Inan, a passionate, intelligent, talented man who gave me so much, but did not live long enough to allow me time to provide him anything in return.

To my mother, Nazmiye Inan, a strong, tenacious, hardworking woman who has always demonstrated great leadership, a positive attitude, and absolute dedication to her children.

MEASURING THE SUCCESS OF YOUR WEBSITE

A CUSTOMER-CENTRIC APPROACH TO WEBSITE MANAGEMENT

HUROL INAN

Copyright © 2002 Pearson Education Australia Pty Ltd

First published 2002

Pearson Education Australia
Unit 4, Level 2
14 Aquatic Drive
Frenchs Forest NSW 2086

www.pearsoned.com.au

Acquisitions Editor: Nella Soeterboek
Project Editor: Kathryn Fairfax
Cover and internal design: Ingo Voss of Voss Design
Copy Editor: Ross Gilham
Indexer: Russell Brooks
Typeset by Midland Typesetters, Maryborough

Printed in Australia by Griffin Press

1 2 3 4 5 06 05 04 03 02

ISBN: 1 74009 648 7

National Library of Australia
Cataloguing-in-Publication Data

Inan, Hurol.

Measuring the success of your website : a customer centric
approach to website measurement.

Includes index.

ISBN 1 74009 648 7.

1. Internet marketing. 2. Web sites – Design. I. Title.

658.8002854678

An imprint of Pearson Education Australia

FOREWORD

The need for a more formal approach to web metrics is becoming very clear. Two recent anecdotes illustrate the problem well.

In recent discussions with one of our clients, the marketing director expressed the strong view that his firm was interested only in 'known' users of its website. This was a B2B ('business-to-business') product information initiative with no online sales. The client's strategy was to create reasons for visitors to identify themselves (login) and was adamant that if the firm could not get metrics about visitors—who they were and where they were spending their time—the site was of no value. 'If I can't measure it, I can't respond to it!'

The CEO of another business on the point of rebuilding their web site expressed it differently. 'Imagine if one of our executives came to me with a proposal to print a colour magazine about our products each week and suggested that we should staff up an editorial department to author this magazine and print by the thousands, and then leave it in public places—at airports, at railway stations, and on street corners. But, according to this proposal, there would not be any feedback, and no one would be able to tell us what products or articles people found interesting or how long they spent reading about them. We would say that our executive was crazy and show him the door. But that's how dumb I feel our first website was.'

The message is clear—capturing the metrics around online behaviour is the key to increasing the value of a web initiative. This is true in all styles of website from B2C (business to consumer) to B2B (business to business), from online market to online community, from intranet to extranet. Although the web holds the promise of fine-grained, high-value feedback on customer behaviour and trends, its potential will not be realised without a clearer grasp of the fundamentals of web metrics.

<

Against this background, this book is very timely. It goes to the heart of the issue of how enterprises can begin to understand what happens when people interact with their sites. Logically set out and illustrated with numerous helpful case studies, the book provides a practical framework for the emerging discipline of web metrics. Managers who follow the approaches described in this book will fundamentally transform the way they plan and develop their web initiatives. This book will help managers evolve their websites towards ever-increasing relevance and value, based on actual measurement of what works and what does not.

I warmly commend this book to all those interested in learning about this emerging subject—thus optimising their web initiatives, and the returns to be gained from them.

Michael Kean
Senior Strategy Partner
Deloitte Touche Tohmatsu
Sydney, Australia

CONTENTS

ACKNOWLEDGMENTS

The encouragement, support, and contributions of many people made this book possible. I extend my thanks to them all.

To Mark Neilson, my dear friend and work colleague for continually providing encouragement and support, and for investing so much of his spare time to reviewing, discussing, and correcting every aspect of the manuscript. I am deeply indebted to you, Mark. Thank you.

To Michael Kean, my boss and mentor at Deloitte and Eclipse, for inspiring me to take on new challenges, for extending his help whenever I need it, for reviewing the first draft of the manuscript for this book, and for providing the generous Foreword. I learnt so many new skills from you, Mike. Thank you.

To Nella Soeterboek, my publisher for accepting my book proposal, for having confidence in me, and for providing guidance throughout the process. You opened a new door for me, Nella. Thank you.

To Chris Wilson, my close friend, for listening to me at any time, and for providing huge encouragement and support while I was writing this book. I appreciate your friendship and all your help, Chris. Thank you.

To Esra Hekimoglu, my close friend for 'cracking the whip' to keep me writing, and for providing assistance during the contractual arrangements. You helped me stay on track, Esra. Thank you.

To Vanessa Rowe, my colleague at the Eclipse Group for providing feedback on the book, and for finding original names for the fictitious case study examples. I appreciate your contribution, Ness. Thank you.

ACKNOWLEDGMENTS

To Ross Gilham, my editor, for reflecting his passion for the English language in his work on my book. You improved the clarity of this book, Ross. Thank you.

Many thanks also to Hilary Weiser, Peta Neilson, Rebecca Campbell, James Breeze, Adrian Giles, Andrew Brown, Amit Sharma, Eugene Tan, Nur Dikmen, and everybody at the Eclipse Group.

ABOUT THE AUTHOR

After eleven years of management and technology consulting with Andersen Consulting and Deloitte Touche Tohmatsu, Hurol Inan has recently moved into freelance eBusiness consulting. His consulting work primarily focuses on strategy and planning aspects of eBusiness initiatives.

Hurol frequently speaks at industry events and has published many articles in both print and online media. He covers topics such as the use of Internet technology as a business enabler, the measurement of the effectiveness of web applications, and the impact of the Internet on the business community and the general community.

Hurol is currently an adviser with the Eclipse Group in Sydney, Australia, providing expert advice on interactive strategy, design, and implementation to Eclipse and their clients.

Recognised as an authority in this important and rapidly expanding field, Hurol Inan can be contacted via his website at <www.hurolinan.com>, where all current contact details can be found.

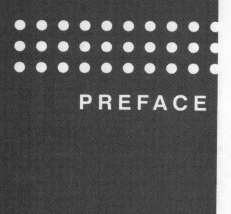

PREFACE

Can you confidently say that your website is working? With the huge proliferation of websites in recent years, it is not surprising that many sites are not working. The 'Internet rush' has resulted in websites being created too fast and without careful planning. People are learning their lessons the hard way, and often too late, and these failures could be avoided.

If you build a website, you must have a solid reason for doing so. Once the website is operational, it is crucial to understand how well it works—failure to do so is a waste of time and money. Building, operating, and maintaining a website—or any other eBusiness initiative—requires money. And like any other investment it should provide a tangible investment return.

So how do you get the payback?

The only way to know if you are getting return on investment is by systematically tracking and analysing your website. In other words, you need to measure it. Not only does this provide you with a verdict on your site's success, but also it offers insights into the site's function so that you can respond to issues in a timely manner.

We have come a long way since the early days of the Internet. The hype surrounding our discoveries and mistakes over the past few years has helped us to build awareness of the medium and its uses as a conduit for business. With this knowledge, organisations are now better positioned than ever to leverage the benefits of the Internet in their business practice.

One of the big lessons we are still learning is that organisations should not build websites with the aim of increasing hits, page-views, and unique sessions. Rather, the website should focus on serving the organisation's customers and on achieving returns for its investors.

This book provides a practical and sensible approach to implementing web-measurement practices. It will enable you to:

- determine how well your website meets the needs of your online customers;
- understand how well your website helps customers successfully interact with your business;
- confirm how well the benefits identified in your business cost/benefit analysis are being realised; and
- identify what changes are required to make your website more successful for both your customers and your business.

This approach is applicable to both existing websites and to the blueprints of sites you plan to develop in the future.

Using the knowledge gained from this book, organisations can be confident that their websites are working.

INTRODUCTION

OBJECTIVES OF THE BOOK

To establish how successful your website is, you require the knowledge and the techniques that will enable you to measure that success. This book provides that knowledge and those techniques.

The primary objectives of this book are:

■ to establish the need for measuring the success of websites;
■ to define a common, but customisable, framework for measurement; and
■ to advise on the implementation of practical and sensible measurement practices.

The book aims to measure the success of websites by closely examining the interactions that occur between your customers and your website, and by identifying ways of improving these interactions. The process demands a more intimate understanding of customers, and this book will help you to develop this understanding. By reading this book, you will gather the knowledge that will help you get to know your customers and, more importantly, keep them coming back.

AUDIENCE FOR THIS BOOK

If you are investigating ways to maximise the success of your online initiatives, this book is written for you.

You will have already recognised the strategic role that eBusiness initiatives play within your overall business strategy. This book will take things a step further, by delivering the mindset, knowledge, techniques, and solutions that are required to commence implementing measurement practices and, ultimately, to improve the degree of success. Any organisation that uses the web to communicate with its customers, business partners, and employees can benefit from this book.

However, this book is not intended for website-administration purposes. Although it does contain some level of technical information, it is intended only as a guide in establishing the realm of possibilities in data collection and analysis.

PURPOSES OF CHAPTERS
Part 1 A customer-centric framework
Chapter 1 Measuring success
This chapter:

■ establishes the need for, and the importance of, being able to say that your website is working;
■ discusses the dangers of using basic metrics (often provided by standard reports from website-traffic analytical tools) as a measurement tool; and
■ introduces the concept of measurement by systematic tracking and analysis of the performance of a website.

Chapter 2 Defining a framework
This chapter:

■ builds a common framework that sets the scope and focus of measurement activity;
■ demonstrates that customer-centricity is the key to a successful eBusiness venture (and thus is paramount to measurement practices);
■ discusses the importance of understanding customers and what this means in the eBusiness arena;
■ provides a set of generic stages for engaging with customers as the basis of the framework;
■ completes the framework by introducing and discussing the implications of possible dropouts from different stages of engagement (and the factors that are likely to cause these dropouts); and
■ verifies the suitability of the framework by providing case studies from four distinct (fictitious) websites.

Chapter 3 Applying the framework
This chapter:

■ describes how to apply the measurement framework to various situations;

■ argues that an organisation's eBusiness initiative is now an integral part of the entire business strategy, and that it should integrate with, or at least influence, the offline processes and channels; and

■ demonstrates how the framework operates in these more complex situations.

Part 2 Metrics, analysis, and interpretation
Chapter 4 Engaging customers

This chapter:

■ discusses each stage of customer engagement (*reach*, *acquire*, *convert*, and *retain*);

■ provides generic metrics to measure the effectiveness of online and offline initiatives to enhance the engagement; and

■ introduces analytical techniques to explain the underlying reasons for performance and to identify items for practical action to improve performance.

Chapter 5 Explaining dropouts

This chapter:

■ discusses dropouts from normal customer engagement (*leakage*, *abandonment*, *attrition*), and provides generic metrics; and

■ introduces analytical techniques to explain the underlying reasons for dropouts and to identify items for practical action to improve performance.

Chapter 6 Containing dropouts

This chapter:

■ discusses the major factors that influence dropouts (content appropriateness, design effectiveness, and website-performance efficiency), and provides generic metrics for these factors; and

■ introduces analytical techniques to explain these factors further and to identify items for practical action to improve performance.

Chapter 7 Choosing metrics and analytical techniques

This chapter:

■ discusses the importance of selecting the appropriate metrics and analytical techniques for a particular website;

- defines the factors that influence this selection process;
- discusses the importance of setting targets; and
- explains that some metrics might have a limited lifespan and interdependencies.

Part 3 Data collection, cleansing, and integration
Chapter 8 Understanding the data
This chapter:

- introduces the data required to calculate metric results and to perform further analysis;
- discusses new measurement units introduced by the Internet, and the lack of standard definitions for these measurement units;
- presents different layers of technology that can be used in websites, and the data that can be collected from these layers; and
- discusses the importance of how webpages are served as a foundation for understanding collected data about user activities on a website.

Chapter 9 Collecting the data
This chapter:

- introduces user identification as the primary mechanism for linking measurement data;
- discusses the different techniques used to identify the users of a website and illustrates situations in which each technique is suitable;
- defines the data-collection points for user-activity data, discussing data elements that can be collected, and the implications of choosing each collection point; and
- discusses the privacy implications of data collection.

Chapter 10 Preparing the data for analysis
This chapter:

- stresses the importance of using quality and consistent data to produce meaningful results;
- advocates the removal of various types of non-qualifying user-activity data;

- defines the data elements (from offline sources and other online sources) that might be required to integrate and consolidate with user-activity data, providing a checklist for conducting this task; and
- advises on how to deal with large volumes of data.

Part 4 Implementation of web measurement
Chapter 11 Resourcing web measurement
This chapter:

- defines human-resource requirements for web-measurement practices; and
- argues that this is a formal role that should be conducted by web analysts.

Chapter 12 Selecting tools and vendors
This chapter:

- specifies the requirements for technology solutions;
- provides guidelines for selecting tools and vendors; and
- provides reasons for different solutions providing different figures.

Chapter 13 Implementing measurement practices
This chapter provides an iterative approach for implementing web-measurement practices within an organisation.

Chapter 14 Predicting the future
This chapter makes predictions for the future of web measurement.

TERMINOLOGY USED IN THIS BOOK
Several terms are used frequently throughout this book. These terms have been chosen purposefully, even though there are other words that could have been chosen in their places. These terms are defined below, together with reasons for preferring their use.

eBusiness, Internet, websites
Since 1990, when the World Wide Web brought electronic business into

the spotlight and increased its commercial popularity, the web has become ubiquitous in most modern information systems. It is important to note, however, that *electronic business (eBusiness)* goes beyond the *Internet* and World Wide Web. It also encompasses the use of other media for the exchange of business data between computers—including automatic teller machine (ATMs); Internet-enabled devices such as mobile phones and personal organisers, and Internet protocols such as email and chat.

This book applies to all eBusiness media. However, to simplify the context and discussions, *websites* will consistently be used as examples. This focus is due, among other things, to their widespread use, and to ongoing confusion concerning the accurate measurement of their success. The book thus generally uses websites as representative of all eBusiness media, but when the discussion does not apply to other media, this is noted as appropriate.

Customer, client, audience, user, visitor

The terms *customer*, *client*, *audience*, *user*, and *visitor* have distinct meanings.

- *Customer* implies previous transaction(s) with the business to purchase goods or services.
- *Client* is a person or a firm that procures professional services.
- *Audience* represents a group of people for whom the website is built.
- *User* is a person who uses a website.
- *Visitor* is the person who visits a website.

All of the above terms apply at some stage or another to most people. However, as this book is primarily written for business managers who use eBusiness initiatives in dealing with their customers, it is clear that the customer is the key focus. It is the person as *customer* whom organisations try to *reach*, *acquire*, *convert*, and *retain*. The term *customer* is therefore widely and purposefully used throughout this book.

Enterprise, business, organisation, company

These terms have similar meanings and are easily confused.

- *Enterprise* is a business organisation that is willing to undertake new ventures and initiatives.

- *Business* implies a commercial focus.
- *Organisation* is a broader term reflecting structure and governance, but not necessarily having a commercial focus.
- *Company* is a business enterprise that is formed as an association among people.

Because the concepts discussed in this book can apply to any organisation that engages with its customers through eBusiness initiatives—not necessarily requiring or implying commercial arrangements—the term *organisation* is used most frequently throughout this book.

Web measurement, website-traffic analysis, Internet-traffic measurement services

Web measurement is defined in this book as the process of measuring the success of an individual eBusiness initiative. This definition is broader than *website-traffic analysis*. *Website-traffic analysis* examines the flow of visitors to a website, from when they enter the site until they leave it. Some authors refer to this as *site-centric analysis* or *clickstream analysis*.

In addition to *website-traffic analysis*, there are *Internet-traffic measurement services*. Companies that offer these services focus on measuring the overall traffic flowing on the Internet, and ranking the target destinations of this traffic. Both *website-traffic analysis* and *Internet-traffic measurement services* are useful in discussions of web measurement. However, the web-measurement discussions in this book go beyond traffic analysis to measure what matters for the business.

CASE STUDIES USED IN THIS BOOK

Four generic examples are used as case studies throughout this book. Although they do not introduce any new concepts, they are used to provide real-life examples for the themes discussed. They serve to verify the concepts and to facilitate implementation of them.

These case studies have been chosen carefully to cover a wide spectrum of issues faced by business today. As you read them, you might want to apply the same concepts to an eBusiness initiative with which you are familiar. This should help you to challenge and fully grasp the concepts.

The case studies appear throughout the book in the style illustrated below.

CASE STUDY EXAMPLE 1
Pandora's Online Grocery

Focus

A fictitious online grocery, Pandora's Online Grocery, is used to illustrate discussions that focus on websites targeting consumers to buy physical products (often commodities and consumer products) on a frequent and regular basis.

Rationale

A grocery is a fine example of such a business. As consumers, we buy groceries frequently and regularly (usually on a weekly basis or more often), and the total cost of purchases is not usually very expensive.

This website service is about using the online channel as opposed to visiting a physical grocery shop. The implication of using the service is that our spending on groceries usually remains the same. Over the last few years many people have grown accustomed to these services, and we often see delivery vans from these services in our metropolitan areas and suburbs. At least we are all familiar with what to expect from these services.

Features

The grocery featured in this book, like the other case studies, is fictitious. It represents the online arm of a bricks-and-mortar chain that was operating well before the Internet was developed. Such businesses offer their full catalogue online and provide next-day delivery. In addition to shopping-cart functionality, they offer several features to make it easier for customers to purchase groceries, as well as seeking other avenues to appreciate and enhance the loyalty of their online customers.

Like services

Any website that you visit frequently and regularly to make purchases could be a business model that is similar to this grocery. Such businesses might include online music shops, online bookshops, online stock-trading services, and even online travel companies.

Concepts illustrated

CASE STUDY EXAMPLE 2
Stinger's Online Cars

Focus

Stinger's Online Cars is used to illustrate discussions of websites that target consumers who are considering the purchase of an expensive product, and who will not need to buy a similar product for a long time.

Rationale

A car manufacturer is a good example of such a business because a car is an expensive purchase and, once bought, is usually kept for three to five years.

Features

The fictitious car manufacturer discussed in this book uses its website to showcase vehicles, to generate prospective leads for its dealership network, to sell direct to customers, and to enable after-sales service and support. The consumers' relationships with the manufacturer and other parties—such as dealers, service providers, insurance companies, and finance companies—change significantly during different stages of the purchase and ownership process. This presents opportunities and challenges for the car manufacturer to keep the online services relevant to the consumers' needs.

Like services

Businesses of a like nature include any organisations that target consumers with relatively expensive, infrequently purchased items, and that make use of online channels in their interactions with consumers. These might include computer hardware and software vendors, home-appliance manufacturers, and manufacturers of electronics and hi-fi equipment.

Concepts illustrated

Concept	Chapter	Page
Verifying the stages of engagement	2	18
Dropouts from engagement stages	2	21
Customising the framework	2	24
Enabling cross-channel travels	3	30
Making insurance payments	3	39
Using web-customer profiles for more targeted reach	4	55
Retention is a step towards loyalty	4	74
Combining user-identification techniques	9	168
Integrating data from customer-interaction points	10	195

CASE STUDY EXAMPLE 3
Agora's Online Marketplace

Focus

This case study is used to illustrate discussions of online marketplaces that offer businesses the ability to participate in the marketplace to sell and/or buy products and services.

Rationale

Online marketplaces operate with business models that are distinctly different from the other case studies provided in this book. They target business *users*—both buyers and sellers—as opposed to *consumers*. The decision to participate in a marketplace is a more formal and strategic decision for business users than that of a consumer deciding to shop online. This example contrasts the measurement requirements of an online business initiative, as well as illustrating how the discussions apply to these initiatives.

Features

The case study features an independent marketplace that brings together buyers and sellers to trade in various forms—such as requests for tender, auctioning, and catalogue sales. The participants are required to register to use the marketplace.

Like services

Businesses of a like nature include any organisation that has web applications targeting business users. Such a business will benefit from the concepts illustrated in this case study.

Concepts illustrated

Concept	Chapter	Page
Dropouts from engagement stages	2	21
Using acquisition features to increase conversion likelihood	4	59
Detecting changes in relationship from frequency of online activities	4	78
Maintaining relevance by onsite search-effectiveness analysis	6	111
Customised content for marketplace participants	6	112

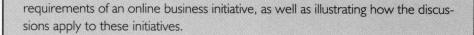

CASE STUDY EXAMPLE 4
Vault's Information Portal

Focus

This case study is used to illustrate discussions of websites offering information services to consumers.

Rationale

The differentiating feature of this example is its focus on delivering *service*, as opposed to *physical products* involving close integration with external logistics systems and services. The web has created the opportunity for many information portals to bring individuals together around a common interest or goal. These portals have a unique business model, based on *content brokerage*.

Features

This case study features an information portal that offers various levels of information content, directory services, and interactive features. It might or might not be affiliated with an offline product (such as a newspaper or magazine), and requires subscription (either pay or free).

Like services

Businesses of a like nature include any organisation that provides significant volumes of online content—from pure play companies to organisations such as newspapers, magazines, broadcasting companies, and professional services firms.

Concepts illustrated

Concept	Chapter	Page
Separate websites for registered and occasional users	3	37
Multiple conversions	4	63
Containing leakage by path analysis	5	94
Containing leakage by multi-dimensional analysis	5	95
Timespan of content relevance	6	110

ACCOMPANYING WEBSITE

This book is accompanied by a website that contains information which is subject to change. This includes vendor details, reviews of commercially available solutions, links to other articles and resources, a dictionary of web-measurement terms, and so on.

Throughout this book, specific references are made to the website (type the locator code, where available, on the website for quick access to these content areas). However, it is expected that the website content will evolve as the subject matter develops—making it possible to communicate new knowledge to readers as it becomes available.

Visit the website now at <www.hurolinan.com> to bookmark it or add it to your favourites, and refer to it frequently for additional information while reading this book.

PART

1

**A Customer-centric
Framework**

CHAPTER

1

Measuring Success

Recent years have seen a rush to invest heavily in Internet technologies. Many factors have contributed to the rush—such as the influence of financial markets, the expectations of customers and, more significantly, the fear of lagging behind. The legacy of this rush is a proliferation of websites— many of which are not working or not delivering the expected results. Unfortunately, people are not investigating the reasons for these failures.

It was distressing to learn recently that the website of a very large multi-national was virtually running on its own. Forget about having sensible measurement practices in place! No one was even looking at the basic traffic reports!

In another example, a high-profile Australian travel company was claiming significant volumes of online business. Initially, they wanted a counter on each page to measure the site's success. However, when the possibilities of what can be measured were explained to them, they realised that there is more to web measurement than counting the number of times that the pages have been displayed.

Think about your online initiatives. Can you confidently say they are working, and that they deliver value to your target audience and your business?

Before we look at how successful your site is, we must go back to basics. If you are building a website you need a good reason for doing so. Then, once it is operational, it is critically important for you to understand how well it is working for you. Unfortunately, attracting users to a website is a difficult and expensive task, whereas losing them is very easy. After all, the competition is only a mouse click away. Unless your website gives your potential customers what they are looking for, and does so in a clear and simple fashion, they will look elsewhere. The only way to know if you are operating in the right way for your customers is by systematically tracking and analysing the traffic on your site.

LEARNING FROM BAD PRACTICES

Many website operators do not even take the time to look at basic traffic reports. There is little awareness about the possibilities of website-measurement practices and what they can provide to a company. Indeed, too many people are still ignorant of the potential of the medium as a space within which to learn more about their customers.

A mistake that many people still make in measuring the success of their websites is correlating its success with basic metrics—such as unique sessions served and page-views displayed. In reality, organisations should not build sites with the aim of increasing unique sessions and page-views. Rather, their website should focus on serving their customers and achieving returns for investors. Not only are these basic metrics meaningless, but also they can lead to incorrect interpretations, bad decisions, or no decisions at all. They cannot tell you if your online initiative is successful or not.

Many organisations recognise the potential of web measurement, but are still confused about it. As a result, people are investing in technologies without fully understanding the capabilities of such technologies, or the results they can deliver.

Software vendors and service providers have jumped on the measurement band-wagon, offering solutions that rely on the standard metrics. The vendors try to sell their solutions on the basis of these metrics, propagating the notion that web measurement is limited to such standard measures.

It is important to dispel this myth, because standard metrics address only some aspects of web measurement. Without the proper context, they can lead to incorrect conclusions. The examples below illustrate this.

- High traffic volumes to a certain page might indicate that the page is well received. However, the traffic might be on a circular navigation path, or the page might contain so many keywords that search engines have indexed this page better than others.
- You might notice that your customers are not purchasing on the website, but prefer to go to your bricks-and-mortar business. This might lead to your making a decision not to promote your products at all on your website—even though the customer might have first seen the product online, and might have been motivated to buy it at that point.
- Information gleaned from a measurement firm might show that average total time spent on your website is lower than that of your competition. However, this information might, in fact, mean that your website employs a better infor-mation architecture, making it easy for users so they don't need to spend as much time on it.

■ Online pricing information might seem to be popular because of the high number of visits. As a result, your organisation might decide to publish more detailed price information. However, a more detailed analysis might reveal that most of the information is being downloaded by your competition.

UNDERSTANDING THE POSSIBILITIES

Any measurement practice should start with an understanding of what is achievable in the medium. So what is possible for measuring the success of your website?

The web is the only communication channel that allows you to track and analyse practically everything that your customers are doing as they interact with your business. Furthermore, this happens in real time, which means you can collect, analyse, and respond to these data immediately and accurately. In a bricks-and-mortar business environment, it is not practical for a salesperson to follow every customer through the building, tracking his or her movements. On a website, however, you have the ability to monitor your customers in a new and empowering way. Here, you have the opportunity to see which products they are considering, so that you can move in to close the sale, or up-sell, or cross-sell, as appropriate.

You can also use this real-time information—about how products and services are selling—to test the market with new products. For example, you can prelaunch a new line of products on your website and then use web analysis to see how customers respond. This takes much less time and money than doing the same marketing test in the physical world, where collecting (and analysing) data is a comprehensive process. Online, products can be positioned with different marketing campaigns that change by the hour, instead of by weeks or months.

Customer and sales data collected from the web can be integrated with information from the organisation's other customer-interaction points. This unified, cross-channel view of customers can be used to deliver more personalised services to the customer, whether it be at the call centre, through direct mail, or via the website itself.

Proper analysis of the interactions between your customers and your website will tell you more than whether your website is designed well. It also offers valuable insights into the real motivations and behaviours of your customers, because people tend to be true to themselves when surfing the Internet. Furthermore, proper analysis can provide you with important information that can be used to predict the likely outcome of future activities, such as product launches.

Using your website for the opportunities highlighted above puts you in an ideal position to learn more about your customers and their needs. The question of what to look for when analysing the performance of your website depends largely on what aspects of customer interactions you would like to find out about. It is then possible to gauge these against what the online initiative is built for. This will help you improve the customer experience and obtain maximum return for your initiatives.

TAKING A SENSIBLE APPROACH

If your business has an operational website, you are strongly advised to ask yourself a number of questions:

- Are the user activities on your website being analysed?
- If so, are they being analysed by people who are qualified to do so?
- Is *meaningful* information about your online customers being gathered?
- Is this information being used to influence how you run your business in areas such as product development, customer relationship, and customer service?

Measurement of your online initiatives is a vital component of the management process. In a nutshell, it is about collecting, analysing, and interpreting data to answer the following questions:

- How do the customers arrive at your site?
- Which customers use the website?
- How do the customers interact with your site?
- What was the result of the visit? Did it have a happy ending?

The results of such an analysis should help you to understand and retain your online customers.

This book provides a practical approach to the implementation of web-measurement practices. It will enable you to see how well your website is meeting the needs of your online customers, to understand how it facilitates interaction with your business, to confirm how well the benefits identified in the business case are being realised, and to identify what changes are required to make your online initiatives more successful. Furthermore, this approach is applicable both to existing websites and to the blueprints of sites that you plan to develop in the future.

And the result will be that you will be able to say, with confidence, that your website is working.

SUMMARY

If you build a website, you must have a solid reason for doing so. Once the website is operational, it is important to understand how well it is working and how it contributes to your overall business strategy. Failure to do so is a waste of time and money because the construction, operation, and maintenance of a website (or any other online initiative) requires capital. It is no different from the other investments that an organisation makes, and it should always be subjected to an appropriate business cost/benefit analysis.

To date, there has been little awareness of web-measurement practices and their possibilities for businesses. Associating the success of a website with basic metrics—such as unique sessions served, and page-views displayed—is a common mistake. In reality, organisations should not focus on increasing unique sessions and page-views. Rather, they should aim to serve their customers well and, ultimately, to make a profit. Not only are basic metrics meaningless, but also they can lead to incorrect interpretations and decisions. Such basic metrics cannot tell you if your online initiative is successful or not.

The web is the only communication channel that allows us to track almost everything that customers do during their time on your site. Although it is a difficult and expensive task to attract customers to your site, losing them is easy. The retention of customers should therefore be a priority. Systematically tracking and analysing your customers' interactions on your website, and acting on the results, will increase the chances of customer retention.

CHAPTER

Defining a Framework

2

In the brief history of the commercial Internet, web-measurement companies have focused their attention on the success of online advertising. Not only did advertising enter the realm of eBusiness before other business processes, but also it had measurement models that were tried and true, and that could output return on investment from various communication channels (from print media to television).

Traditionally, the advertising industry, although assuming responsibility as the initial point of contact with the public, has also acted as a 'buffer' between its clients and their new customers. A distinct time-lag exists between a potential customer's exposure to a company's advertising and that customer's first visit to the company's bricks-and-mortar business to make a purchase.

The Internet has changed this. Enterprises have suddenly found themselves either one click away from, or face to face with, their customers, and are discovering new ways to reach potential customers directly. Many have attempted to destroy their value chains by going direct to consumers, and many have experienced cannibalisation of their channels along the way. And most of them have failed, or are experiencing great difficulties, in their attempts to move closer to their customers via the Internet. Many factors contribute to these failures, the underlying factors being a failure to justify investments with sound business assessment, and a failure to measure the success of these initiatives to ensure a return on investment.

The temptation to use advertising metrics to measure the success of eBusiness is understandable, given the key role that advertising plays in the traditional economy. However, these standard advertising metrics are not fully transportable to eBusiness for two reasons.

■ The metrics focus on maximising the return on *advertising*, but use of the web has progressed beyond advertising to cover *all* aspects of business. To get a complete picture, there is a need to measure all components of online activity.
■ The metrics are designed to measure advertising *events* or *campaigns*, which are predominantly one-off or short-lived activities. eBusiness, on the other hand, is *ongoing* and requires continuous tracking and measurement.

With this in mind, there is an urgent need to formulate a holistic approach for measuring the success of eBusiness initiatives. It should encompass metrics for *all* facets of online activity, and should continually provide the information needed for a thorough understanding of what is happening in the online world to ensure that investment matches return.

This chapter introduces a framework for such a holistic approach, with a particular focus on the importance of the customer. It centralises the customer to measure how well his or her needs are met through your online activities, and it provides indicators that will flag when you might be off-track.

ESTABLISHING THE NEED FOR A FRAMEWORK

A framework can be defined as a fundamental structure for enclosing a set of concepts, assumptions, and practices, designed to simplify the way in which we view reality.

If you are serious about measuring the overall success of your online initiative, you must build a suitable framework within which to conduct your measurement. This framework should clearly set the boundaries and scope of measurement, and it should enable you to verify that the measurement approach is complete and balanced.

If you do not build a framework, your measurements are likely to be inaccurate. Even if you do have a set metrics to measure, without a framework you will have no way of knowing whether these metrics address all of your concerns, whether they are consistent with each other, whether they measure every aspect of the initiative in a balanced fashion, and whether they are, in fact, overlapping (by measuring the same things with different methods).

A well-built framework will ensure that you don't measure things that you don't need to measure, and that you are capturing the information that you intended to capture. In other words, a framework is essential to know what to measure.

BUILDING THE FRAMEWORK

Knowing your customers

To succeed in today's competitive business environment, it is clear that organisations must be customer-centric. To achieve this, organisations are shifting the focus away from internal activities (such as product development and operations) and, instead, are concentrating on strengthening customer relationships.

This 'customer revolution' is continually evolving, with some companies having been quick to pioneer customer-centric practices through effective use of the Internet. Because the Internet provides easy access to product information, prices, product reviews, rating systems, and other data points that enable consumers to make more informed decisions, it has become a valuable tool in building customer relationships. In turn, customers are becoming more empowered and are demanding customer-centricity from any organisation with which they interact.

This move to customer-centricity is a paradigm shift, with many benefits to customers and businesses alike. Organisations that exploit this phenomenon and get closer to their customers are set to reap substantial benefits.

To become customer-centric, an organisation must know who its customers are and what their needs are. In an offline environment, collecting this information requires difficult, costly, and time-consuming market research. eBusiness makes understanding your customers—the essential prerequisite to a customer-centric business—an easier, less costly, and real-time process.

But, even with the Internet, how well do we know and understand our customers? Unfortunately, many organisations have obtained customer information but then not been able to decipher it to get a clear view of their customers. For example, larger organisations might have many pockets of information about their customers in each departmental unit, but no easy way of identifying common customers across the business. And even when common customers can be identified, each department often holds different, and inconsistent, data about the same customers.

A study conducted by Meta Group in March 2000 revealed statistics showing that organisations have a long way to go in understanding their customers.[1] In the survey, completed by 800 business and IT executives, 83 per cent of respondents answered 'no' to the fundamental question, 'Does your company know who the customers are?'. It also found that 67 per cent of respondents did 'not agree' that their companies are effectively using client data to understand their customers. But efforts are intensifying to get to know these customers—56 per cent of Meta Group respondents ranked 'customer intimacy' as a top-three priority within their company.

Understanding your customers delivers a number of benefits, including:

- leveraging existing capabilities better by matching your products and services to the customers' needs;
- designing more suitable products and services according to the customers' needs; and
- reducing the cost of selling, and developing a more targeted reach as a result of a better fit between their needs and your capabilities.

Getting to know online customers

For your online initiative to deliver the benefits of customer-centricity, you have to ask three key questions about your customers:

- Who are they?
- What are their needs?
- What sort of online behaviours do they exhibit?

To answer these questions, you need to really get to know your customers and make your relationships with them more intimate.

Many organisations find the first two questions (above) easy to answer, because they have already gathered a lot of information about their existing customers offline. This can work in your favour, because you can use this knowledge to engage these customers in your online services.

The last question (above) is more difficult to answer because it involves under-standing the behaviours of customers in online channels. The Internet is a relatively new medium and, consequently, not much information exists about user behaviours. Where information does exist, anomalies appear. Although online behaviour reflects what users like and dislike—apparent from their navigation through your site—behaviour is also influenced by the site's design and the features offered for navigation and interaction. Two people with completely different motivations for visiting your site might exhibit very similar online behaviours. Conversely, two people with the same needs might exhibit completely different online behaviours. One might respond well to impulse-buying 'click-throughs', whereas the other might completely ignore them. One might choose to use the buttons to access the featured items or recommen-dations; the other might follow the hierarchical menu to reach the same item. One might visit the site at the weekend; the other might come to the site during working hours. These sorts of differences highlight the wide variation that exists in online user behaviours.

The framework used to measure the success of online initiatives should recognise customer-centricity, and should help organisations to answer, in a practical and useful way, the three questions posed above.

Purpose and audience
For a website to be healthy, it must have a purpose and be directly targeted towards a specific audience. You cannot have one without the other. Think of the purpose as your 'breathing apparatus' and the audience as 'the oxygen in the air'. If there is a failure in either your breathing apparatus or your oxygen supply, you eventually suffocate. You need both to stay alive. A website presents the same scenario. It needs to have a purpose that is relevant to, and well appreci-ated by, its target audience group. Any problems with either its purpose or its target will diminish its success.

Each website carries a unique purpose. This is a natural extension of the variations among different companies. The purpose of your website depends on how you want to use the Internet to improve your business processes and how you want to communicate and interact with your customers, business partners, and employees. There are as many different solutions to these decisions in online business as there are in the offline business world. An organisation might choose to web-enable a whole range of processes such as product design and development, demand-generation, order-fulfilment, customer service, internal financial and human-resource management, and productivity-related areas (such as online workplace solutions). The choice of process that is to be web-enabled, and the way in which it is web-enabled, will lead to great variations in the purpose of the website, and thus make each website unique.

Given this great variation, we cannot say that a website's purpose provides the much-needed common factor for measurement that we are looking for.

So let us now consider the audience. A website must reach its target audience if it is to fulfil its purpose, and this leads to a common process. All customers or potential customers go through the same stages as they engage with a website, from (i) initial attraction and recognition that the website meets their needs; to (ii) the transaction process (whether it be buying a product or exchanging information in return for a service); and, ideally, (iii) repeat transactions. Audience *engagement* therefore provides the common framework for measuring the success of websites.

This model shows strong resemblance to the customer lifecycle concept. eBusiness is customer-centric and measuring its success should also be a customer-centric activity.

Required attributes of the measurement framework

The framework required to measure the success of online initiatives should focus on the performance of organisations in *engaging* with customers online— whether the activities carried out to facilitate this engagement process are conducted online or offline.

It is very likely that an online initiative will not satisfy the requirements of *all* of its target audience, and this can cause some members of your audience to exit your site. This leads to either lost business or duplicated costs, whereby the customer rings the call centre or visits a retail outlet to complete the transaction. The framework should be able to detect these defections when they occur, quantify their impact on the business, and explain the factors that might have caused them.

In light of this, the measurement framework should have three layers:

■ stages of customer engagement;
■ dropouts from engagement stages; and
■ factors influencing dropouts.

The rest of this chapter explains these layers of the measurement framework in detail.

DEFINING THE FRAMEWORK

Stages of customer engagement

In *engaging* with customers, organisations go through a series of unique stages, with each stage aiming to strengthen the relationship further. Generic stages in this process are illustrated in Figure 2.1 below.

The definition of each stage depends to some extent on the reason for engaging the customer in the first place. Therefore, the names given to stages might change accordingly.

The value of the customer to your business increases substantially as that customer progresses up the engagement ladder, and your ability to facilitate this journey is a key success indicator for your online initiative.

Reach

Applying the stages in customer *engagement* to a website (see Figure 2.1), *reach* is your first consideration. As the operator of the website, your organisation will employ different communication channels to reach your target audience. You should develop messages designed to persuade the members of the audience that your website will meet their particular needs—whether it be paying a bill, buying a gift for a special occasion, communicating with like-minded people, or gathering information about the news, a special event, or products and services. Everything you do to get the attention of the various members of your target audience, and to inform them of what your website can do for them, will influence the *reach* of your site.

Figure 2.1 Stages of customer engagement

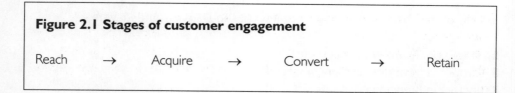

Reach   →   Acquire   →   Convert   →   Retain

Acquire

A successful outcome of the *reach* stage is that members of your target audience visit the website. Once potential customers visit your site they enter the *acquire* stage. In other words, these are all the people who have come to your website based on your promise, and who have therefore given you a chance to deliver on that promise.

Convert

Some of the people who have reached the *acquire* stage will see a match between their needs and what is offered by your site. They will proceed with purchasing, or will comply with whatever else the website is trying to achieve.

This stage is referred to as the *convert* stage, because it involves *conversion* of some sort—such as buying a product, registering to become a member of the site, downloading a white paper, and so on. This stage involves positive action by the customers. They are no longer merely surfing. In performing this action, customers have invested something of themselves in your website, and can therefore be considered *converts*.

There are many potential points of *conversion* on a single website, and each can represent a different value for the organisation. This differential value should be reflected in the overall measurement framework used to measure the success of your website.

Retain

If the customers have a positive experience in the *convert* stage, and if the website has made an impact on them, they might return when they have similar needs in the future, or when they have other needs that they have noticed your website could address. This is regarded as the *retain* stage, and the quality of experience in this stage reflects the customers' trust in your website, and their loyalty to your business.

Throughout these four stages of engagement (*reach*, *acquire*, *convert*, and *retain*), your company is likely to use the website as the primary medium of interaction. You can also perform several offline activities that serve to enhance the customer experience, and therefore accelerate the engagement process.

CASE STUDY
Stinger's Online Cars
Verifying the stages of engagement

The customer's knowledge of a particular make or model of car might come from various sources—such as a friend's recommendation, an advertisement in the media, or noticing the car in question in traffic. Some of these sources are associated with the different *reach* techniques utilised by Stinger's Online Cars, whereas others are less directly influenced by the company. For the people who are contemplating buying a new car, *all* of these sources influence the *reach* that Stinger has towards them.

If the potential customers decide that they like the model, and if they go to Stinger's website to find out more about it, they enter the *acquire* stage. At the website, the visitors can look at specifications, pictures, pricing, and other information about the car. If they like what they see, they might want to take the next step—in most cases a test drive. They can use the dealer-locator functionality on the website to find their nearest dealer and make an appointment online, or they can simply turn up at the dealer for the test drive. In taking this action, they have just entered into the *convert* stage.

Let us assume that they buy the car. In a few years' time, if their experience with the car has been good, and if they are considering upgrading to a newer model from the same manufacturer, they might return to Stinger's website. At this point they have entered into the *retain* stage for Stinger's Online Cars.

Revisiting the full *engagement* process (Figure 2.1, page 16), you will notice that, as customers move from one stage to the next, their value as customers increases substantially.

DROPOUTS FROM ENGAGEMENT STAGES

It is clear from the discussion above that the effectiveness of the *reach* stage represents the potential for the website, and the success of the *convert* and *retain* stages translates into bottom-line results for the business. There will inevitably be *dropouts* when moving from one engagement stage to another, and these dropouts impact on your website and your bottom line. This section deals with these dropouts.

Dropouts can occur at any stage of the engagement process. The implications of these dropouts for your business will differ, depending on the stage at which they occur. Obviously, the cost associated with dropouts increases substantially if they occur in deeper stages. This cost has two components—the opportunity cost incurred by the business because of the dropout (thus involving loss of potential revenue), and the costs involved with managing and containing them smoothly. The difference in cost between dropouts of one stage compared with another can be substantial, and they are therefore treated separately. Figure 2.2 (below) places these dropouts on the framework introduced earlier in Figure 2.1 (page 16).

Leakage

Leakage happens before any serious engagement with potential customers takes place. The situation is analogous to that of window shoppers who stop in front of a retail outlet, browse the window displays, and then walk away without entering the premises. The ratio of *leakage* to *acquisition* represents the effectiveness of your *reach* techniques in bringing the right audience to your website, and illustrates how well your value proposition—as presented by your website—appeals to the needs of customers attracted by your reach technique.

Leakage also represents customers whom you were able to *acquire*, but whom you were not able to *convert* (see Figure 2.2). The cost of leakage is usually lower than other types of dropout. Similarly, reducing leakage and transferring the customer to the next stage in the engagement process is easier than for subsequent stages.

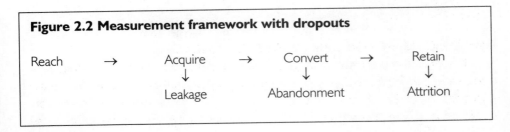

Figure 2.2 Measurement framework with dropouts

Reach	→	Acquire	→	Convert	→	Retain
		↓		↓		↓
		Leakage		Abandonment		Attrition

Abandonment

Abandonment describes the dropouts at the next stage in the process of engagement. A common form of abandonment is demonstrated when customers fill their 'shopping cart' at a consumer website that sells physical goods, but do not commit to the final purchase. In a bricks-and-mortar retail situation, if customers walk into a shop, examine the merchandise closely, make enquiries about price and availability (perhaps negotiate, as is common in some cultures), and then decide not to proceed with the purchase, they have abandoned the engagement process. An analogous situation exists with online abandonment. For abandonment to occur, the *convert* stage needs to have started.

Attrition

Drop out at the final stage of engagement is called *attrition*. This occurs when a customer has had successful engagement with the website, and has been in the *convert* stage at least once, but decides to go elsewhere for subsequent needs. Examples include the changing of a subscription for Internet access from one provider to another, or the buying of books or CDs from one online outlet, and then proceeding to buy these goods from another online retailer. Among the various types of dropout, attrition represents the greatest cost to your business.

The characteristics of *leakage, abandonment*, and *attrition* become clearer when we consider examples from three of our fictitious case studies.

CASE STUDY
Pandora's Online Grocery
Dropouts from engagement stages

Leakage for Pandora's Online Grocery is represented by the people who have visited the website but who, for some reason, decide not to buy any groceries. The implications of *leakage* are significant in this type of business, because buying groceries is a mundane task and most people would not have come across such grocery sites by accident. We can assume that visitors to online grocery outlets have a genuine need for groceries and have intended to use the service.

Abandonment in this case is represented by someone filling up a shopping cart but exiting the site before completing the transaction.

Attrition occurs when someone who has bought from the online grocery at least once, stops coming back for new grocery purchases.

CASE STUDY
Stinger's Online Cars
Dropouts from engagement stages

Leakage for Stinger's website occurs when a potential customer visits the site at least once—often many times—but does not progress any further towards *conversion* (that is, the making of an appointment with the car dealer for a test drive).

Abandonment in this case can be manifested in various ways. For example, customers might make an appointment but not turn up to test drive the car, or they might complete the test drive, negotiate a price (and perhaps even order the car), but then exit out of the full *convert* stage before completing the purchase. There might therefore be multiple steps towards full conversion, and many organisations consider *each* of these as conversions and measure them separately.

Attrition for Stinger's Online Cars occurs when a person currently owning one of his cars decides to replace it with a car from another manufacturer.

CASE STUDY
Agora's Online Marketplace
Dropouts from engagement stages

For Agora's Online Marketplace, *leakage* equates to potential buyers and sellers coming to the website, gathering information about how it works and what it has to offer to them, but never signing up to use it.

The types of *abandonment* depend on what the marketplace considers its *convert* stage to be. A buyer who places a request for quotation but cancels it before appointing a supplier is an example of such abandonment.

Attrition happens when the buyer stops placing any more requests for quotations, or when the seller stops responding to requests for quotations on the online marketplace.

FACTORS INFLUENCING DROPOUTS

The major factors influencing dropouts include:

■ content appropriateness;
■ design effectiveness; and
■ website-performance efficiency.

This is illustrated in Figure 2.3 opposite.

Content appropriateness

Content appropriateness entails accurately meeting the content needs of your target audience, in terms of both relevance and quality. Increasing this variable assists in transferring your customers from one stage to another, and will lessen the likelihood of dropouts.

Design effectiveness

Design plays a key role in delivering your promises to your audience. Whether you use text, pictures, audio, video, or other formats, to be effective your site's design must match the online behaviours of your target audience. Design incorporates presentation and navigation. Ease of use and simplicity are the keys to effective design.

Website-performance efficiency

The technical performance of your website reflects its *efficiency* which, in turn, is a key to retaining customers. From the point of view of customers, performance is assessed on how quickly the pages are downloaded into their browsers, the availability (or uptime) of the site, and the number of errors on it.

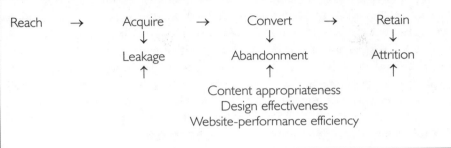

Figure 2.3 Measurement framework with dropout factors

Reach   →   Acquire   →   Convert   →   Retain

↓   ↓   ↓

Leakage   Abandonment   Attrition

↑   ↑   ↑

Content appropriateness
Design effectiveness
Website-performance efficiency

In trying to create visually attractive websites, it is easy to forget about page download-times, which are critically important for customers using slower modem connections. You might have the best content and design in your market but, if your site is slow, it will frustrate your customers and they will go elsewhere. Remember that your competition is only one click away!

CASE STUDY
Pandora's Online Grocery

Factors influencing dropouts

A mismatch of *content* and the communication message at the website will cause *leakage*.

For instance, imagine that Pandora's Online Grocery has run an advertising campaign promising one-hour delivery for groceries but, when customers visit Pandora's website, they find out that the one-hour delivery is only for specific metropolitan areas and is available only during specific hours of the day. In this situation Pandora has a *content* mismatch that is very likely to cause significant leakages from its website.

Likewise, poor *design* of the shopping cart or product-locator features on its website can cause *abandonment* due to frustrations in using the site.

These three factors (*content*, *design*, and *efficiency*) go hand in hand. Needs guide the *content*; behaviours guide the *design*, and technical performance (that is, *efficiency*) is the basic requirement. Your ability to produce appropriate *content* and effective *design* depends to some extent on how much you know about the behaviours and needs of your target audience. Sacrificing one of these factors for any of the others will reduce the overall effectiveness of your website and will cause dropouts. In contrast, improvements in all three factors will increase your chances of transferring customers from one stage to another.

CUSTOMISATION OF THE FRAMEWORK

The framework outlined above is generic. It can be specified and customised to a particular business or website. Organisations in particular industries might go through *sector-specific* stages that are well defined for that sector. In these circumstances, you might consider using such specific stages instead of the generic ones.

Therefore the stages of engagement (Figure 2.1, page 16) might differ for customers from one segment to another. For instance, the differences in managing the customer engagements of dealers, as distinct from retailers, can be reflected in the framework.

CASE STUDY
Stinger's Online Cars
Customising the framework

Stinger's Online cars might choose more specific terms for the stages—such as 'awareness', 'consideration', 'shopping', 'ordering', 'ownership', or 'fan club'. The website functionality can be designed in close collaboration with overall business strategies to address each of these stages.

When mapped to the generic framework, 'awareness' and 'consideration' would fit in the *acquire* stage, 'shopping' and 'ordering' in the *convert* stage, and 'ownership' and 'fan club' in the *retain* stage.

By customising, Stinger manages these stages separately, and measures the success of functionality offered for these stages individually.

The emphasis placed on the various individual stages in the engagement process might also change from one business to another. The *retention* of customers, for instance, might not be an issue in a given business. Rather, the focus in this business might be on servicing the existing customer base with the least possible cost. If this is the case, you might, for example, choose to rename the 'retain' stage as 'support'. A case study further examines this in Chapter 3 (page 41).

It is advisable to consider the business environment that your organisation is in, and decide if there is a need to customise the framework. However, regardless of your particular circumstances, the principles of the stages set out in the framework still apply.

SUMMARY

A frame of reference provides the essential guide for your web-measurement activities, enabling you to set parameters and make decisions on the results. It requires a common framework that clearly sets the boundaries and scope of measurement. A good framework should give you confidence that your measurement approach is thorough and balanced.

It is important that your framework is customer-centric. It should measure how well organisations engage their customers and validate how well the online initiative meets the needs of customers. This relies on knowing who your customers are, and understanding their needs and online behaviours. The framework has three layers.

- The first layer measures the effectiveness of a website during the customer *engagement* process.
- The second layer identifies undesirable *dropouts* from the stages of *engagement*, and targets users who are leaving the website through *leakage*, *abandonment*, and/or *attrition*.
- The third layer classifies *content appropriateness*, *design effectiveness*, and *website-performance efficiency* as the factors that cause these dropouts.

This framework will be further considered in the following chapter, when it will be applied to various working examples.

CHAPTER

3

Applying the
Framework

We have come a long way since the early days of the Internet. The hype surrounding our discoveries and mistakes over the past few years has helped to build awareness of the medium and its uses as a conduit for business. We are seeing various working examples of this. Most of these examples are not stand alone—they are embedded in the way that organisations do business, and form an integral part of business practices.

Internet technology can be used to facilitate and enhance many of the interactions that take place between an organisation and its customers, its partners, and its employees. The principles discussed in the previous chapters, taken together, form the cornerstone of this facilitation—an online initiative must engage and empower its audience to be successful.

In this chapter, the measurement framework introduced in Chapter 2 will be applied to four real-life situations. These situations represent proven and distinct uses of the Internet. They are:

∎ integrating online and offline channels;
∎ implementing multiple websites;
∎ providing point-in-time services; and
∎ using online and offline channels concurrently.

Each of these subjects is considered in turn in this chapter.

INTEGRATING ONLINE AND OFFLINE CHANNELS

A common observation by analysts is that customers who use multiple channels to interact with a retailer tend to spend more money with that retailer than do customers who interact via a single channel. Meta Group reported on J.C. Penney's 'three-tail strategy'—which integrates web, store, and catalogue shopping channels.[1] According to the report, online shoppers spent an average of US\$121 per year, catalogue shoppers spent US\$194 per year, and retail-only store shoppers spent US\$194 per year. Customers who used all three channels spent more than US\$1000 at J.C. Penney each year.

Analyst reports, and the websites of data-mining product vendors, are full of case studies that illustrate similar results. Customers prefer to interact with businesses across multiple, integrated channels, and will reward the businesses that offer this by increasing their spending on purchases. Armed with this knowledge, organisations should integrate online and offline channels, encourage their customers to use all available channels, and allow them to move fluidly from one channel to another. This strategy maximises the lifetime value of customers.

Drivers for cross-channel travels

We all know of excellent websites that offer customer self-service. You can visit these sites and answer your own questions quickly and efficiently. My own web-hosting company has such a facility—where you can log problems or enquire about the service. But the first thing that I always do when my website is down is pick up the phone and call. I want to learn about the problem and receive assurance that they are working on it before I start waiting for the fix. It is my personal choice—my preference—to use the phone as a medium of interaction in this situation. (However, when I want to make enquiries about some of their other services, or when I am seeking resolution of a non-critical problem, I am happy to use their online service.)

The reason that I reach for the phone in certain situations is that the web does not allow for the emotional persuasion that is an essential element of certain types of interaction. In many cases, customers want to know that their requests are being personally attended to. Customers therefore sometimes prefer to use the phone when the Internet is apparently so quick and easy.

Martin Lindstrom, in *Clicks, Bricks & Brands*, takes the argument further— probably too far. He says that the web appeals to only two of our five senses— sight and hearing. He then goes on to argue the need for synthesising other sensory appeals: 'The online marketer's role will be to help the consumer smell with the eye, taste with vision and feel with sight'.[2] Although this first assertion hits home in seeking to achieve such outcomes, designers need to beware of overstretching their creativity and producing sites that forget their original purpose. The web essentially deals with only sight and hearing. What is required of website operators is an intelligent recognition of the capacity and limitations of these senses in helping your customers make informed decisions, analyse data, and conduct transactions. If your customers' decision-making processes require other sensory input, customers should be able to turn to your other channels to experience such input.

Purchases, particularly by first-time buyers or by people who have experienced problems with your business in the past, are loaded with unknowns. These customers want to ask questions and seek assurance. Therefore, it is common to see customers seeking face-to-face interaction by visiting a physical retail outlet at some stage of the engagement process. This helps them to make final decisions and to feel comfortable about the purchase. When trust is established with your product and company it is easier for your customers to consider the online channel as an exclusive medium for *future* engagements. When you feel confident that you have their trust, you might even encourage customers to move to the web channel by clearly communicating the advantages (the 'value proposition') of using this medium.

The desire of customers to travel among various channels is thus natural. Allowing customers to do this is a good practice and can help transfer more customers deeper into engagement with your organisation.

Influencing cross-channel travel decisions

Although it is ultimately up to the customers to decide how and when they want to travel among various channels, an organisation clearly has preferences as to which channels it uses to communicate with customers. There are significant costs involved with operating each channel, but redirecting customers to another channel simply because it is more convenient for you is a bad strategy for any organisation that values its customers. Before a redirection strategy is adopted, your organisation should seek to understand *why* your customers have established preferences with particular channels. Equipped with this knowledge, you can then enhance the channels and devise incentives that encourage your customers to travel in the preferred path voluntarily.

Banks provide an excellent example of this. Today, there are many people who would never consider walking into a bank unless they have a complex transaction to complete. Instead, these people seek out the nearest automatic teller machine (ATM). The task of convincing a large percentage of the world's population—all the people who hold bank accounts—that ATMs are more

Case study
Stinger's Online Cars
Enabling cross-channel travels

On its website, our fictitious car manufacturer, Stinger's Online Cars, can provide several features that assist customers in choosing their new car. These include sections on performance, style, financing, and insurance. By choosing the functionality most relevant to their needs, customers enter more deeply into the *acquire* stage. Once customers have established the suitability of a car, they are ready to take the next step—usually a test drive.

Stinger's Online Cars can facilitate this by providing a dealer locator. This functionality finds a dealer in close proximity to the customer and books the test drive. By doing this, Stinger migrates the customer from the online channel to an offline channel.

The customers test drive the car and, if they decide to proceed with the purchase, the dealer inputs them into Stinger's website as being 'car owners'.

The website might then offer several features that help the customers maintain their car—such as arranging services and answering technical questions. By entering the new customers on Stinger's website, the dealer migrates them *back* to the online channel.

convenient, was a more difficult task than that faced by most organisations. Despite the size of the target audience, and the cultural and financial diversity within this audience, the banks have succeeded in making ATMs the most common method for making withdrawals across the globe. Banks are now promoting online banking of all types, already with significant success. They provide incentives—such as favourable fee structures for online transactions, and the convenience that comes with around-the-clock, location-independent banking facilities. Most importantly, the banks are attempting to ensure that consumers are happy with what these facilities are delivering.

Some organisations might implement strategies to use certain channels exclusively for different stages of the customer engagement, and attach strong value propositions to these stages. For instance, they might choose to encourage an initial face-to-face interaction to ensure suitability of their products, with subsequent interactions then taking place via other channels. The cost of selling the initial product in this case might be higher, but the likelihood of retaining the customer over an extended time increases. By influencing cross-channel travel decisions, these organisations maximise the return on their customer-engagement strategies.

Measuring online and offline channels together

If your customers can travel among channels, it is not enough to measure the success of your online channel alone. This gives you an incorrect representation of reality, and can be misleading.

For example, you might make the judgment that your website is unsuccessful because nobody has been making purchases online, even though the functionality to do so is available. If you do not know exactly what has happened when a customer has visited your site, you cannot assume that your assessment is accurate. It might be that a customer has visited your website to learn about your products, has spoken to your call-centre representatives for more information, has compared your products with those of your competitors and, finally, has placed the order at a retail outlet—whether it be your own shop or that of a reseller.

Discounting the role of your website in these interactions is a misjudgment. If your website did not exist, your customers might not have chosen your product at all, or they might have spent longer talking to sales representatives at your retail outlet—which would mean that the final outcome rests entirely on the persuasive abilities of your employees. In the above scenario, with a functioning website, customers were mostly convinced that this was the right product for their needs, and have gone to the retail outlet to convince themselves fully and/or simply complete the transaction.

Cross-channel travels between online and offline media can be incorporated into the measurement framework (as introduced in Chapter 2, page 9). It is quite

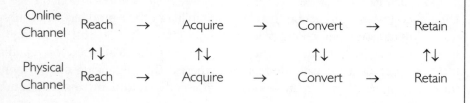

Figure 3.1 Travelling between two channels

possible that customers will move among multiple channels—such as branded retail outlets or resellers, brand-specific websites, resellers' websites, kiosks, call centres, and other Internet devices. Figure 3.1 above illustrates how these situations can be incorporated into an extension of the model originally presented in Figure 2.1 (page 16).

It is clearly evident that integrating data from multiple channels and using such data to support and strengthen customer interactions—throughout the organisation and within its various channels—is fundamentally important. A customer's overall satisfaction level is defined by an organisation's weakest channel. A website might be award-winning, but it is not the only channel that customers use. Someone who loves the website, but has a bad experience at the call centre, goes from being a potential customer to a lost one.

What do the above discussions tell us? Organisations must understand how the online and offline channels interrelate and support each other during the engagement of customers. This requires an identification of when and where cross-channel travels occur, and the integration of all interactions from multiple channels for an overall assessment.

Layers of measurement
The success of a website should:

▪ first be measured individually; then
▪ be measured within the context of the organisation's channel strategy; and, finally,

Pandora's Online Grocery

Integrating customer and sales data

Our fictitious online grocery service, Pandora's Online Grocery, integrates all customer and sales data from online and physical outlets. Integrating this information allows Pandora to monitor and predict how customers interact between channels. This includes an understanding of how customers combine the channels to get what they need. What do they purchase online compared with what they purchase at a physical retail outlet? This knowledge can be used to target offers of specific products via a particular channel to certain customers. The result is that Pandora's Online Grocery has information that it can use to run its business more profitably, while the customers receive better service.

In addition to analysing how its existing customers shop, Pandora must also make predictions about its future customers—what (and how many) products they will buy, how they will find out about these products, when they will buy them, and even where new physical retail outlets should be located.

The goal of Pandora's Online Grocery is to understand its customers and their needs better, so that it not only provides the products they need, but also supplies those products within the right channels.

∎ be measured within the context of overall business strategy.

If you do not include all of these aspects in your analysis, it is impossible to understand the true contribution of your website to the overall success of your business. See Figure 3.2, page 34.

Web measurement should be performed first because it identifies a specific set of actions needed to enhance the customer's experience.

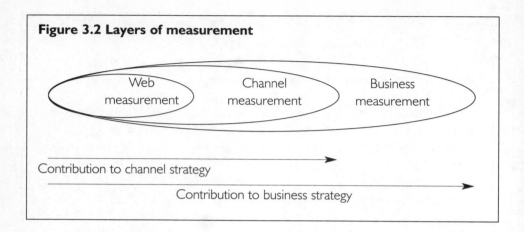

Figure 3.2 Layers of measurement

Next, measurement within the context of the channel strategy reveals how a particular website supports customer engagement across channels. This analysis should show channel-share percentages, influences, and cross-channel referrals, as well as pinpointing any cannibalisation issues. Breaking the analysis down into customer segments and product groups can lead to an effective customer/product/channel-mix strategy, the results of which offer answers for influencing the cross-channel travels of your customers.

Finally, measurement within the *overall business context* reveals the relative contribution of the website to the business, and will tell you if the website was a wise investment.

IMPLEMENTING MULTIPLE WEBSITES

At the beginning of this chapter, four proven and distinct uses of the Internet were introduced. The first of these (considered above, page 27) was the *integration of online and offline channels*. Now we turn to the *implementation of multiple websites*.

For various reasons, many organisations have multiple websites. This could result from branding strategy. It could be in response to the diverse requirements of different target audience groups. It could be due to distinct differences in the products and services on offer.

CASE STUDY
Buying a Hewlett Packard printer

Does Hewlett Packard (HP) know that I visited its website many times before eventually buying a printer from one of its resellers?

Recently, I needed to replace my old printer with a new one—one that would print faster and not jam papers and cause unnecessary frustrations. From my existing knowledge of printer brands, and what I had picked up from other people, it wasn't difficult to create a shortlist of three printer manufacturers.

I started my shopping on the Internet. First stop was the manufacturers' websites to find out about the product options. At one stage, I had the websites of all the manufacturers open, while I read specifications and compared them.

After browsing the websites and gathering information, I had a clear idea of the suitable products from each vendor. Then I wanted independent advice.

I first visited the ZDNet website. Previous experience with this site meant that I could trust the objectivity and comprehensiveness of its product comparison service. Following a quick stop at ZDNet, I decided to buy an HP printer. I went back to the HP site to read the specifications one more time. To validate my decision, I sought other people's experiences of this printer model by typing the model number in the WebFerret consolidated search engine. Nothing appeared in the search results as negative commentary on this product. My research had taken an hour and I was now ready to buy the product—thus entering the *convert* stage (see Figure 2.1, page 16) at the HP website.

My goal now was to buy the printer at the cheapest price available and have it delivered as soon as possible. I took a note of the price and delivery lead-time, if I were to buy the product online direct from HP. Then I went to the websites of a number of e-tailers that sell electronics, noting down price and availability information from each company. Finally, I rang my local department store and established that it had the product in stock. I went to the department store that afternoon and bought the product there. Although it wasn't the cheapest option—despite the store lowering its price when advised of the prices from other retailers—I preferred this option because I was able to use my department store credit card. Use of this card extends, by a year, the warranty period of the purchases I make.

I picked up the printer and brought it home for installation. One of the brochures included in the box was the product registration form. With this form, the manufacturer was advising me to register my new printer at its website, as well as enticing me with a chance to enter a cash prize draw. I did register, although unfortunately I didn't win the prize!

To summarise my printer purchase, I bought an HP printer and the HP website helped me with this purchase. I visited it many times as it repeatedly served my needs, and it facilitated my choice of a suitable printer. And HP knows this because I registered my purchase at the website.

What could HP have done differently? Two things caught my attention during the experience, neither of which stopped me from purchasing.

First, its website has a poor navigation system for first-time users. As a shopper who is not very familiar with HP products, I circumnavigated the site a few times before I could find which printers would meet my needs.

Second, although HP's knowledge of my purchase is vital when assessing the success of its website, the only way that HP knows of my purchase is through my voluntary registration. HP could have trained the sales representatives at the department store to take me through the website and register my product.

Separate websites for customer segments

Many consumer product companies establish separate websites for recognised brands or for different consumer segments.

The age of a consumer is often a determining factor in this decision because it affects aspects of online behaviour and brand association. For example, older

---

CASE STUDY
Vault's Information Portal
Separate websites for registered and occasional users

Our fictitious information portal, Vault's Information Portal, might implement multiple websites to meet the different needs of registered users as distinct from unregistered, occasional visitors. This offers a distinct benefit in that the additional volume of traffic resulting from the unregistered visitors does not affect the performance of the site for frequent users.

It might be that occasional visitors to Vault's Information Portal get lesser services on a time-delayed, semi-dynamic site, whereas the registered users get real-time data access and better service.

---

consumers of a brand of soft drink might value this product for its refreshing flavour. Younger consumers of the same drink, on the other hand, might value its association with sporting and outdoor activity.

The manufacturer of the soft drink might choose to leverage both of these associations by establishing separate websites—each appealing to one consumer segment. If this strategy is adopted, the result will be two discrete online channels with very little opportunity for cross travels. The two websites should be linked because each contributes to the success of the same product. The company should retain confidence in the strategy of linking the websites because the net contribution of both websites, working in concert, will be greater than the contributions of the two websites acting independently.

Various websites from the one organisation facilitate a number of desired outcomes through different functionality. Although these outcomes are often the same across the sites, the specific functionality offered on each site (to support these outcomes) might be different. This is the point at which the organisation can combine and compare the success of each website. *Aggregation* is possible and useful here because each site targets a discrete audience, but offers similar or identical products. It is highly unlikely that data are

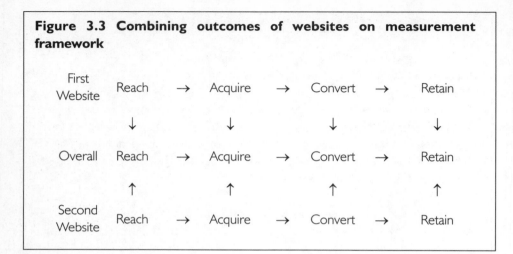

Figure 3.3 Combining outcomes of websites on measurement framework

recorded twice, because potential users are likely to use only one of the possible websites. Figure 3.3 (above) shows how the outcomes from each website can be combined on the measurement framework. The figure shows how the metrics from different websites should be integrated to assess the overall customer engagement.

Separate websites for product groups

Larger companies offer a wide spectrum of products and services, and use separate websites for groups of products. Take Microsoft for example. With msn.com, through an information and lifestyle portal, the company sells various non-software consumer products, many of which come from affiliated companies. The only mention of Microsoft appears in the 'Links and Resources' page of the msn.com website, and when a user clicks on this link they are transferred to the Microsoft product site.

The concept of *aggregation* suggested above (page 37) would not be appropriate here because *different* products are being sold, potentially to the same customers. The measurement practice should, instead, focus on the interactions between these sites. This is the same as the traditional concepts of cross-selling and up-selling, and the same principles apply directly to the online channels.

PROVIDING POINT-IN-TIME SERVICES

Having considered two of the four proven and distinct uses of the Internet (*integration of online and offline channels*, page 27, and *implementation of multiple websites*, page 34), we now turn to the *provision of point-in-time services*.

Increasingly, business strategies are recognising the value of the Internet as a tool for providing customers access to specific processes such as event-driven services. This is a smart move, because these applications use the strong attributes of different channels to enhance customer engagement and experience, offering convenience and efficiency.

Point-in-time services occur when customers are directed to your website to perform a well-defined task at a specific, often event-driven, time. Examples include payment for utility bills, product registrations, technical support,

CASE STUDY
Stinger's Online Cars

Making insurance payments

Our fictitious online car manufacturer, Stinger's Online Cars, could provide a point-in-time online service for insurance payments. For customers who have bought car insurance from Stinger's online service, an automated email system might send payment notices twelve days before the due date. The customers could go to Stinger's website or to the websites of their various banks to make the payment via one of the payment methods provided.

Similarly, when the insurance policy is due for renewal, Stinger might mail a printed copy of the new insurance policy and send reminder emails to the customers. On receipt of these, the customers could go to Stinger's website to renew their insurance policies.

By web-enabling insurance payments and policy renewals, Stinger's Online Cars will achieve transactional efficiencies as well as offering convenience to customers.

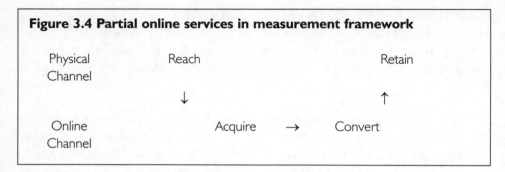

Figure 3.4 Partial online services in measurement framework

Physical Channel	Reach		Retain
	↓		↑
Online Channel	Acquire	→	Convert

customer satisfaction surveys, voting, and data collection for utility bills (such as gas-meter readings).

Figure 3.4 (above) shows a diagrammatic representation of point-in-time online services in the measurement framework.

As illustrated in Figure 3.4, the customer is reached as a result of an event in the physical channel (that is, the offline world). The *reach* technique triggers the need to visit the website to perform a specific task, such as paying a bill. At this point the customer enters the *acquire* stage, and performs the task. Dropouts might still occur during the *acquire* and *convert* stages—usually as a result of negative experiences during these stages.

Some point-in-time online services can be repetitive, requiring frequent visits to a particular website. In such cases, repeat users are expected to enter directly into the *convert* stage.

A common trait for point-in-time services is that the website does not focus on *retaining* customers. Rather, retention, and indeed the overall relationship, is managed offline.

Measuring success
The key focus of the business case in point-in-time services is the cost savings that result from using the Internet service, as opposed to using other channels. The transaction efficiencies offered by a website can far outweigh the efficiencies of other methods. However, success is still dependent on the organisa-

CASE STUDY
Making payments online for traffic infringements

A motorist has received a traffic infringement notice. He goes to a website listed at the bottom of the notice to get more details about the offence, and to pay the penalty using his credit card.

This is not a site that should be measured on its 'stickiness'—very few people want to become familiar with this website and become a loyal customer! Indeed, the government department offering the service probably doesn't want visitors to become its loyal customers either. Given this, how does the site provider measure the site's effectiveness? And why would the provider want to measure its success?

If you were the operator of this site—having invested a great deal of time and money in its development—you would want to measure its effectiveness to justify your investment in offering the service. Designing, implementing, and maintaining a website can cost a significant amount of money, especially if integration with other systems is involved. So, even if you do not necessarily want to retain customers, it is important that you can still measure your site's success.

In terms of *reach*, you need to ensure that all offenders know about the availability of this service and that they can be convinced about the convenience of using it. In this instance the primary channel of communication is the infringement notice sent out to the offenders.

It is obvious that the cost of processing the payment is smallest when the offender pays online with a credit card. So, once you have persuaded offenders to use the site to pay their fines, it is important that they do not drop out. This is best achieved through effective content and design, which not only makes it easier to use but also assures users that it is safe to use the service.

Once the offender proceeds to pay the penalty, the interaction enters the *conversion* stage. In this particular case, *retention* is not an issue. What matters is that awareness of the existence of this channel to pay the fine is established, and that it is a hassle-free experience. This should be the objective of the service provider. Note that some people are natural promoters who spread their good and bad experiences to other people voluntarily. All we can hope for, in this instance, is that the offender spreads the good news, reaching other drivers who might be in the same unfortunate situation.

If you are the provider of such a service, you will encounter people who come and check out the site first, and who then return closer to the due date to pay for the offence. How do you track and understand this?

I confess that I have recently had the misfortune of going through this process. Because I was not aware of having breached the traffic law, I first looked at the details of the offence to convince myself that it was accurate. It is important for the website analyser to record this without treating my first visit as an *abandonment*. Indeed, I went back to the site on the due date for payment, and settled my bill.

In an overall context, analysts should be measuring the relative benefits for customers using this service compared to other channels of payment.

This particular example relates to a public service, and ease of access to such services is of paramount importance to the government. The government has a responsibility to service the community. Governments have every right to provide incentives for the take-up of the online channel and to educate the community about the convenience of using such services.

Although the example is not a very pleasant one, I would like to take it one step further. In a wider context, because there is a direct correlation between such offences and the number of accidents on our roads, it is in the interests of the analysts and the government to reduce the number of traffic offences. There exists on the website an opportunity for the operators to use the payment channel to rehabilitate the offenders. The effects of these initiatives can be measured together.

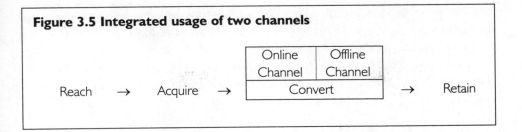

Figure 3.5 Integrated usage of two channels

Reach → Acquire → | Online Channel | Offline Channel | → Retain
with Convert spanning both channels.

tion's ability to encourage its customers to use these services. Therefore, both the effectiveness of facilitating the move to online transactions and the inherent transaction efficiencies should be measured when estimating the business case.

USING ONLINE AND OFFLINE CHANNELS CONCURRENTLY

Having considered three of the four proven and distinct uses of the Internet (*integration of online and offline channels*, page 27, *implementation of multiple websites*, page 34, and *provision of point-in-time services*, page 39), we now turn to the final subject of this chapter—*using online and offline channels concurrently*.

It has already been observed that the use of online and offline channels concurrently is effective in the delivery of various services. Providers of content-rich material adopt this technique to benefit from the strong attributes of online and offline channels in an attempt to engage and interact with customers effectively. Part-delivery of television or radio programs and printed books is a good example of this collaborative approach.

Figure 3.5 (above) illustrates how the concurrent use of online and offline channels fits into our framework.

There are several ways in which you can achieve concurrent usage. The first is by delivering different content pieces in an orderly sequence. Joining an online forum about a current affairs topic immediately after the broadcast of a television program, or taking an online quiz after a reading a chapter of a book, are good examples for this type of concurrent channel usage.

Another type of concurrent usage is simultaneous delivery of content using multiple channels. A good example of this is a popular radio program on science that is conducted by Dr Karl Kruszelnicki on ABC Radio in Australia. The listeners can post questions, reply to each other, or provide real-time comments while the program is on air. 'Dr Karl' (as he is known) reads and responds to these postings as they arrive.

A strategic issue with concurrent channel usage is self-cannibalisation. This applies especially to television programs that divert the attention of viewers from one medium to another, particularly once the program has ended. This means that the television station is potentially losing—from one program to the next—a slice of the audience that it might easily have retained. To date, however, the percentage of viewers participating in post-program online activities is not significant compared with overall audience numbers. Indeed, it might never be a real issue at all—because there is strong evidence that people are multi-tasking when consuming various forms of media. A study conducted by Simmons Market Research Bureau found that its respondents were able to fit in 7.5 hours time spent with media into 4.5 hours of actual time. The same study argued that the heaviest multi-taskers are between the ages of 12 and 34 years, with adults generally multi-tasking slightly more than younger respondents.[3]

Measuring success

Building, maintaining, and operating online channels that can be used concurrently with offline channels is an investment in company resources, time, and money. There should be a sound business case justification before implementing such a strategy. Once the concurrent channels are operational, it is important to measure their success to justify the investment.

The benefits identified in the business case could include:

■ prolonged lifespan of the product;
■ richer content with participation of the target audience; and
■ instantaneous or more timely feedback.

The measurement of success should link directly to how well the organisation delivers on these benefits. The first test is the organisation's ability to promote interest in the online channel while delivering the product on its primary format, and then converting this interest into action on the online channel. The number of customers that it can direct from one channel to another should be part of the measurement. Once the customers are using the online channel, the benefits identified in justifying the investment should be measured to ensure the realisation of those benefits. The generic benefits listed above will be discussed further below. Please note that there might be others specific to your particular application.

Prolonged lifespan of the product
Websites can be used to *prolong the lifespan of the product*. To draw from the examples given above, television programs are restricted by broadcasting times and are often a result of significant amounts of research. By using the website, the program can become available for an extended period of time and act as a reference source for the viewers.

A book publisher can increase the shelf-life of a book by taking out the sections that are likely to change in the future and listing them on the website instead, where they can easily be updated.

Richer content with participation of target audience
A website can be used to generate *additional content through the participation of its audience*. The users can add their views on the concepts and provide additional examples. For the book example, this would mean an opportunity to create new editions of the book with richer and more relevant content. To attract audience participation, its benefits must be clearly communicated to the users.

Instantaneous or more timely feedback
Websites provide an excellent alternative to offline market research, by providing a platform or forum in which customers can *provide their feedback*. Such sites can demonstrate to an organisation how successful its product has been.

CASE STUDY
Online forum for ABC's *Four Corners*[4]

The Australian Broadcasting Corporation (ABC) runs online discussion forums for a number of its programs. *Four Corners*, an investigative journalism program, is an excellent example of how this can work successfully.

This program is the longest-running current affairs program in Australia, having been aired since 1961. It attracts a weekly audience of 700 000 to 1 000 000 people nationally. After the broadcast of each program, viewers are encouraged to enter the online forum to discuss the night's topic and put questions to a panel of independent experts. The forums last two hours, starting immediately after the broadcast of the program, and they enable viewers to read the discussions and post remarks.

These forums attract an average of 400–500 postings a week (from an estimated 200–300 viewers). But the number of postings fluctuates significantly according to the topic of the program. For instance, there were 1353 postings for a program on 'mad cow disease' and 1126 for a program on controversial political figure Pauline Hanson. The highest number of postings has been more than 5000—for a program on asylum-seekers. Total page accesses that week were approximately 450 000, of which more than 390 000 were forum-related. The lowest number has been 67, attributed to a transmission error whereby the online forum was not announced. In that same week, total page impressions dropped to 58 000 from the average figure of 104 000.

According to Hitwise <www.hitwise.com.au>, the ABC website <www.abc.net.au> ranks in the top forty Australian sites by number of visits. The contribution of the forums in attracting traffic to the site is significant. *Four Corners* generates almost half of its page-views immediately after the program, and another 20 per cent on the next day, when the program is aired again during daytime.

What encourages people to join these forums? This is a difficult question to answer for a program such as *Four Corners*. The program covers a broad spectrum of subjects and might appeal to different audiences on each night. A particular program might experience only average television viewer ratings, but then attract huge interest in the forum afterwards. Conversely, a given program might have been comprehensive enough to have answered all the questions for viewers, so they do not need to visit the site afterwards.

What makes the forum successful? The subject matter of the program must invite quality discussion. For instance, the most intelligent and sophisticated debates occur after programs on environmental science—such as water quality, salinity, or 'mad cow disease'. The program on the 'dot com crashes', on the other hand, was like an online chat.

The forums provide the producers with instant feedback about the level of interest that the program has generated, and how engaged the viewers have been. This helps with the choice of subjects for subsequent programs. The forums provide a democratic platform of content delivery whereby members of the audience can contribute their views on a subject, and can attempt to find answers to questions that were not answered in a short 45-minute television program. Furthermore, the website keeps full transcripts of interviews and any other information that the *Four Corners* journalists collected in preparing the program. About twenty journalists work for six to eight weeks to produce each program, and there is much material that doesn't make it to air. If the subject is of interest to particular viewers, there are links from the website to other sources of content on the subject in question. All of this additional content is published on the website with minimal effort, because it has already been gathered for the program itself.

The website extends the availability of the program from only 45 minutes to as many hours as the viewer wants to spend in researching the subject. It also provides a mechanism for making new information available to the audience. For example, there have been instances where members of the *Four Corners* staff have contacted viewers to provide updates on the programs. In another example, an interviewee refused to do an interview before the show was aired, but wanted to have his say after watching the program. The subsequent transcript was added to the website for viewers to read. This effectively extended the lifespan of the product.

It is clear that the website and forums contribute significantly to the ABC's ability to deliver content to its viewers. The forums and the content published on the website are currently an adjunct to broadcast programs, delivering complementary content. The producers expect a closer integration of online forums and the web channel with the broadcast.

SUMMARY

An eBusiness initiative rarely stands alone. It is only one component of an overall business strategy, and is often used to influence, or be integrated with, other online and offline business processes and channels.

When organisations use the web as a separate channel, they must understand how the online and offline channels *interrelate and support* each other during the engagement of customers. This requires the identification of when and where cross-channel travels occur, and the *integration* of customer and sales data from multiple channels into an overall assessment.

Many organisations choose to *implement multiple websites*. Various reasons underlie this strategy—such as differing customer segments and branding strategies. When developing distinct websites for unique customer segments or product groups, the organisation must ensure that the net contribution of these websites is greater than that of an individual website. The focus of measurement for websites that are built for different customer segments should be on how well the site's functionality meets the needs of that segment's customers. Following this primary analysis, all results must be integrated to provide analysis of the overall customer engagement for the product line in question. In addition to measuring the performance of these websites individually, the measurement should also focus on how much these websites contribute to the success of each other in terms of referrals. This is no different from the concepts of cross-selling and up-selling.

Web-enabling a part of a process is also commonly used. These applications provide convenience to the users while achieving transaction efficiencies for the business, and depend on persuading the customer to use the *web-enabled services*. Both the effectiveness of facilitating the move to online transactions, and the inherent transaction efficiencies, should be measured when estimating the business case.

Many businesses are currently experimenting with the *concurrent use of web and offline channels*. Organisations that deliver content-intensive products (such as broadcasting companies and publishing houses) are adopting this approach to exploit the strong attributes of each medium. The measurement approach, like other applications, should test for the delivery of business benefits. The benefits might include prolonging the lifespan of products, enriching content with participation of customers, and obtaining instantaneous or more timely feedback.

P A R T

2

Metrics, Analysis,
and Interpretation

CHAPTER 4

Engaging Customers

As noted previously (see 'Stages of customer engagement', page 16) the customer-engagement process begins with the *reach* stage, when an organisation uses various techniques to reach out to potential customers. If these techniques are successful, people are persuaded to visit the website. Once at the site, visitors have entered the *acquire* stage, at which point it is important that the promise made by the reach technique should match the visitors' expectations. If it does, the users are ready to enter the *convert* stage, whereby they use the website to meet their needs—whether it be to buy a product or to register for membership. Finally, the organisation must make sure that the users' experiences have been good and that they will return—to become, it is to be hoped, loyal users of the site. This is the *retain* stage.

This chapter discusses these stages further, and provides generic metrics and analysis techniques for each. The objective of each stage is to increase the depth of engagement with the customer.

THE REACH STAGE METRICS

Any activity aimed at attracting the attention of the target audience to a website occurs during the *reach* stage. For consumer websites, this might occur through television advertisements, banner advertisements, or word of mouth. For business websites, attention might be attracted by meetings, internal memoranda, or advice notices.

Reaching the right target audience with the right message is essential for success at this stage—and will largely determine whether subsequent engagement stages are reached. Although you might have developed the best communication material on the market, if your website does not deliver on the promise made in this material you will experience large dropout volumes. Reach techniques must reflect the purpose and capability of websites—because anything else misleads people as to the content of the site.

The choice of a reach technique can be dictated by:

▌ an organisation's marketing strategies;
▌ synchronisation with other ongoing activities; and

■ production and execution costs.

To measure the effectiveness of a reach technique, it must be systematically tracked and analysed. Successful *tracking* is predicated on knowing what to track, and then capturing the necessary data. *Analysis* involves the objective interpretation of the data, in order to reveal the exact nature of the reach process and to discern what can be done to achieve better performance.

At this stage of customer engagement, the objective of measurement is to understand how well the techniques employed have reached the targeted customers. This knowledge should enable the organisation to ascertain the level of success that is being achieved, and to feed the findings back into new techniques that are being designed.

To tailor the reach technique further, and to hone the marketing campaign to a target audience, organisations should also *leverage* the data collected on the website—such as the details of interactions with customers, and information voluntarily provided. This information can aid in building the profiles of those customers who are more likely to buy, or who are more likely to engage with your site.

The metrics to measure the success of a reach technique should procure results that enable the evaluation of its effectiveness in terms of number of people reached and the cost compared with other techniques. Results can then be consolidated to demonstrate the overall performance of the organisation in reaching its target customers.

The effectiveness of a reach can be measured by the following metrics:

- the number of people reached;
- the percentage of targeted reaches;
- the percentage of untargeted reaches;
- the cost per day;
- the cost per targeted reach;
- the percentage overlap with active reach techniques; and
- the number of times that a specific targeted customer is reached.

Each of these is considered below.

Number of people reached

The *number of people reached* is a basic measure that represents the number of people who have potentially been reached by the technique during its implementation period. For a television advertisement, this metric represents the number of households who have seen your message based on a program's total number of viewers. For a banner advertisement, this measure is the number of impressions shown to the visitors at a site. For a website sponsorship button, it is the number of unique visitors who visited the site during a specific period of time.

Quantitative data are often available for the potential number of people reached—at least in the form of estimates. But you should treat such estimates with caution, and possibly use a discounted figure. For instance, the total number of viewers for a television program can be obtained with some degree of accuracy, but what is not known is the number of these people who have flipped channels to avoid commercials or who have gone to get a drink when your advertisement was shown.

Percentage of targeted reaches

Let us assume that your target market is the five million scientists who research biological separation. If your advertisement appears in a newsletter distributed to the one million members of a biotechnology online community, you will have reached 20 per cent of the target audience. This metric clearly depends on (i) knowing who you are targeting, and (ii) being able to measure the reach of the chosen technique to this target audience. Depending on how specifically you have defined your target audience, the latter figures may be difficult to obtain. For example, we can assume that a high percentage of a biotechnology online community are scientists researching biological separation, but what if we considered advertising in an industry journal? Would we then be able to make such assumptions?

Percentage of untargeted reaches

It is inevitable that some techniques will reach both the targeted and the untargeted audience. The higher the level of non-target audience reach, the less effective is your reach technique. There are costs associated with managing these unwanted people—for example untargeted enquiries take up valuable customer service time. To avoid this, you might choose to place your online advertisement on a site that employs personalisation and profiling techniques, by which is it possible to be more specific about the sort of people you are trying to reach. Referrals in technical articles are even better, because people would not be reading these unless they have an interest in the topic.

Cost per day

The *cost per day* is a derived metric that is calculated by dividing the cost of the reach technique by its effective duration. Note that the effective duration of each technique differs markedly. For instance, an email newsletter or media release will generate interest for a few days following its release, but is unlikely to attract new potential customers after about a week. In contrast, a listing in a directory will be effective for the life of the directory. The *cost per day*, when used together with the *cost per targeted reach measure* (discussed below), can provide a comparison of the effectiveness of different techniques.

Cost per targeted reach

The *cost per targeted reach* is a derived metric that is calculated by dividing the cost of the technique by the total number of targeted reaches. The cost involves design, production, execution, and servicing. This last component, which is often underestimated or completely forgotten, involves anything that will cost your company extra resources to deal with. For example, if an intervention generates customer queries, the cost of a customer service representative's time in answering such queries falls under 'servicing'. This metric can be used to compare the cost-effectiveness of different techniques.

Percentage overlap with other active reach techniques

The *percentage overlap with other active reach techniques* reveals the overlap that exists when two or more reach techniques are active at one time—because a person can be exposed to any number of these techniques. This is an important metric to set up because it highlights duplicate costs and avoids double counting, thus enabling the organisation to divert the reach resources more effectively. High overlaps might indicate unwise use of resources or narrow coverage. For business-to-consumer websites, the demographics of target customers can be used as a basis of comparing overlaps. Comparing techniques in pairs can also simplify the measurement of overlap.

Number of times a specific targeted customer is reached

Some target audiences will be reached many times via different techniques. This differs from the *overlap* metric in that this one measures the total number of times that the person has been reached. It is possible that an organisation employs a series of sequential techniques to persuade the target customer to visit the website. These techniques might be highlighting different aspects of the website, subsequently building on the messages given to the target customers and increasing their awareness of the site. The target customers can then better match their needs with the promise given in the reach techniques. For business-to-business websites, where the service provider has high levels of influence in the target audience, this metric can be measured more easily.

THE ACQUIRE STAGE METRICS

Having considered the metrics for the *reach* stage (page 54), we now turn to the metrics for the *acquire* stage.

When the target audience has been reached and persuaded to visit a website, the members of this audience enter into the *acquire* stage. The success of the

> ### CASE STUDY
> ### Agora's Online Marketplace
> *Using acquisition features to increase conversion likelihood*
>
> Our fictitious marketplace, Agora's Online Marketplace, uses a number of features to promote the benefits of joining, as well as showcasing its specific functionality.
>
> Promoting the *benefits* can be as simple as specifying them—reductions in supply chain costs, new business opportunities, or real-time transactions, to name a few—and supporting these with quantitative data from client testimonials and analysts' reports.
>
> Features to demonstrate the *functionality* of Agora's marketplace are based on the tasks that buyers and sellers are expected to perform—such as different methods of sourcing products and services. Agora can provide the same or similar material in various formats to match the design preferences of the new acquisitions. These might include a flash presentation, HTML text, or audio recordings. Each feature is specifically designed for new acquisitions and is aimed at converting them to become users of the marketplace. They all conclude by encouraging the user to start the registration process. Their usage and effectiveness should be monitored.

acquire stage is dependent on the success of the reach stage in bringing well-targeted customers to the website. The closer the match between the capabilities of the website and the needs of the customers, the greater the likelihood of success in the acquire stage, and in the subsequent stages (*convert* and *retain*) discussed later in this chapter.

The measurement of the effectiveness of this *acquire* stage relies on:

■ the ability to identify that the visit is made by a new customer to the website;
■ measuring how well the specific functionality encourages the customer to take the next step (the *convert* stage); and
■ capturing the details of how the user is brought to the website so that the effectiveness of the reach techniques can be assessed.

...y to identify that you have a first-timer on the site enables you to treat ...r differently—offering more guidance and assistance than you would ...return customers. This individual treatment will accelerate the path to ...ions. Technical aspects of such *user identification* are discussed in ...r 9 (page 159).

Websites should provide specific functionality for new customers. This promotes the benefits of the site to the customer, demonstrates key functionality to show how the website is best used, and addresses potential questions and concerns that the customer might have before making a decision to use the website. The measurement focus here should be on how effective these acquisition-specific functionality pieces are, and how much you have to spend on them to start converting customers.

The metrics for the acquire stage must also include the ability to pinpoint which reach technique brought the user to the site. Think about your own experiences—there is always a trigger for your decision to visit a website. It is the same for your customers.

The metrics to measure the success of this acquire stage include:

- the number of acquisitions;
- the percentage of acquisitions against all new acquisitions;
- the percentage of acquisitions against all-time acquisitions;
- the ratio of acquisitions to targeted and untargeted reaches;
- the cost per acquisition; and
- the depth of acquisition.

Each of these is considered below.

Number of acquisitions

The *number of acquisitions* is the number of new customers acquired by a reach technique during its effectiveness period. It is important to note that a customer might visit the website many times and still stay in the acquire stage, particularly in the case of websites that involve complex or expensive transactions. To ensure that these repeat visits are not counted as separate acquisitions, it is important to be able to identify these situations. This requires the technical ability of the website to differentiate between first-time visitors and repeat visitors.

Percentage of acquisitions against all new acquisitions

The *percentage of acquisitions against all new acquisitions* is the percentage of customers acquired by a particular reach technique compared with the total number of all newly acquired customers in a given period of time. The time period considered might or might not coincide with the effectiveness period of the reach technique.

Reach techniques themselves, particularly those that bring the customer to your site from other sites, contain information about the customers and their interests. For example, for customers reached through search engines and directories listings, it is technically possible to capture the referring site and the keywords used to locate your website. When customers visit your site for the first time you know nothing about them (except that they are looking at your site). This referring information is important in helping you get to know them, and should therefore be recorded.

Percentage of acquisitions against all-time acquisitions

The *percentage of acquisitions against all-time acquisitions* is the percentage of new customers who visit the website as a result of a reach technique, compared with the total number of customers who have been brought to the site. This demonstrates the overall effectiveness of the reach technique.

Ratio of acquisitions to targeted and untargeted reaches

Untargeted acquisitions must also be measured in the acquire stage. For example, you might be targeting customers in a particular regional area, but the reach technique might be attracting customers from other regions. If you do not have the resources to cope with these additional customers, you really do not want to attract them in the first place.

Although almost every business dreams of growing nationally (and even internationally!), you might not want to do so at this point in time. However, the Internet is global. How do you deal with people who are accessing your site from other geographical areas? How do you handle international enquiries?

Perhaps you might be interested to learn about the interest in your business from other places. We all are. But then you realise that dealing with these acquisitions will be a nuisance for your business because you don't have the resources to service their needs. If this is the case, you should state your position in a diplomatic way on your website, as part of your acquisition functionality. If you don't do this, you will mislead such visitors, and possibly create extra work for your business. This additional work will steal resources that could otherwise be invested more productively elsewhere.

That said, be aware that these visitors might be the same people whom you will be targeting in earnest in two years time!

Cost per acquisition

The unit *cost per acquisition* can be calculated by dividing the total cost of the reach technique by the total number of acquisitions during its effectiveness period. As an example, say you spend $30 000 on an advertising campaign, buying one million impressions, and that it achieves a 0.5 per cent click-through rate, resulting in 5000 visits. Your acquisition cost is therefore $6 per person.

In addition to the cost of the *reach* techniques, organisations spend time and money in producing the *acquisition* functionality on the website. If these costs are significant, they can be added to the consolidated acquisition costs from all techniques. In terms of comparing the techniques, this might not be necessary because this functionality relates to *all* acquisitions regardless of the technique that brings them to the site.

Depth of acquisition

The *depth of acquisition* is the measure of interest shown by the user towards your site during the visits before *conversion*. The amount of time spent on the site, the number of pages visited, and the amount of participation in interactive features, are all good indicators of this. Participation could include functions such as subscribing to your newsletter, posting and answering questions on your bulletin board, or recommending your site to a friend.

The definition of this metric is specific for each website because it relates directly to the acquisition functionality provided on the site. Metrics such as the number

> ## CASE STUDY
> ## Vault's Information Portal
>
> *Multiple conversions*
>
> On our fictitious information portal, Vault's Information Portal, various actions might be considered *conversions*. These include signing up for a free daily newsletter, joining the online discussion forum, clicking on a banner advertisement, or advertising in the classifieds section. Each has a different value attached to it.
>
> Signing up for the daily newsletter increases the circulation numbers of Vault's portal which, in turn, increases its reach to advocate its point of view and enhances its ability to attract sponsorship and advertising revenues.
>
> Clicking on the banner advertisement generates affiliate revenues for the information portal.
>
> Joining the discussion forum generates content and traffic for the website.
>
> Finally, advertising in the classifieds section generates content, and entices other people to visit the site.

of times that a flash presentation has been viewed against the number of new acquisitions could demonstrate interest in this acquisition functionality. Organisations might want to monitor closely the attractiveness of critical functionality pieces.

THE CONVERT STAGE METRICS

Having considered the metrics for the *reach* stage (page 54) and the *acquire* stage (page 58), we now turn to measuring the *convert* stage.

The convert stage brings closure to the objectives of your website, because it represents compliance by the customers in doing what you want them to do. The nature of this compliance depends upon the nature of the website, and conversion therefore means different things for different websites.

It is a two-way process that involves a rational match between the needs of customers and the offerings of the business. We can call it a *rational* match because decisions made online do not involve the degree of emotional contingencies present in face-to-face contact.

Each conversion has a value attached to it, both for the customer and for the business. But this value is not always measurable in financial terms. It could be an exchange of information (rather than money) in return for a service or product. For instance, a conversion might be the registration process on a free information portal, or might be signing up for a free email newsletter.

Most websites have many potential customer actions that can be considered as conversions. Some of these are considered below in case studies of our fictitious websites.

CASE STUDY
Pandora's Online Grocery
Multiple conversions

For Pandora's Online Grocery, *conversions* might include signing up to use the system, purchasing groceries, referring the site to friends, ordering the ingredients for a featured meal, and so on.

Signing up to use the system and purchasing groceries have monetary value attached to them. Referring the site to friends also has a significant value attached to it, because no one recommends something that he or she is not pleased with. Recommendation shows a level of satisfaction with the service, and represents potential revenue from the purchases made by referred friends.

Ordering the ingredients for a featured meal can be seen as an acknowledgment of the usefulness of the recipes provided on the website. It helps the customers to decide what they *could* eat, as well as simultaneously offering the convenience of ordering the ingredients. For Pandora's grocery, the value is obviously in the value of the purchases. But, more importantly, this recipe service might be a tool to *retain* certain customer segments.

Your definition of a conversion might be different from that of your customers. In their eyes, when dealing with an online retailer, conversion does not occur until the goods are received, or until a notice is issued announcing that the goods are on the way.

Metrics to measure the success of this convert stage include:

- the number of conversions;
- the ratio of conversions to acquisitions;
- the ratio of conversions to reaches;
- the cost per conversion;
- the unit value of conversion;
- the net value of conversion;
- the number of visits before conversion;
- the number of clicks before conversion;
- the average total time spent before conversion; and
- online-affected offline conversions.

To understand fully and accelerate the number of conversions, organisations should analyse the path leading to them. The path to conversion is made up of all the activities that encourage the customer to do what the organisation wants them to do. Knowledge of the conversion path can assist in redesigning the content, in making certain messages crisper, and (with more sophisticated sites) in personalising the experience or in offering real-time help when the system thinks the user is having difficulty. *Path analysis* (see page 122) and *usability testing* (see page 129) are two techniques that can be used to analyse the effectiveness of the path to conversion.

We now turn to a consideration of the metrics for measuring conversion (as listed above).

Number of conversions

The *number of conversions* is the total number of conversions for each conversion type. Drilling down from this metric to the reach technique that brings the customer to the site reveals the effectiveness of the reach technique.

Number of conversions per acquisition

As the name suggests, the *number of conversions per acquisition* is the average number of conversions obtained for each acquisition. It applies only to websites that have multiple conversions, each seeking the attention of the newly acquired customer.

Ratio of conversions to acquisitions

Again, as the term itself suggests, the *ratio of conversions to acquisitions* is the ratio of the total number of conversions to the total number of acquisitions. If the website involves multiple conversion points, separate ratios can be calculated. This metric reveals the effectiveness of the acquisition functionality in encouraging the customers to enter the conversion process.

Ratio of conversions to reaches

The *ratio of conversions to reaches* is another self-explanatory term. This is the ratio of the total number of conversions to reaches. If the website involves multiple conversion points, separate ratios can be calculated, which will give you an idea of the more popular conversions and the interests of your customers. You can also calculate separate ratios for targeted and untargeted reaches.

This metric reveals the success of the customer engagement from the initial reach to the convert stage, thus demonstrating the match of the customer's needs and the effectiveness of the acquisition functionality.

Unit cost of conversion

The *unit cost of conversion* can be calculated by dividing the total cost of the reach technique by the number of conversions executed during the effectiveness period of a reach technique. As an example, let us suppose that you spend $30 000 on an advertising campaign, buying one million impressions. It achieves a 0.5 per cent click-through rate, and this results in 5000 visits. If 5 per cent of your 5000 visitors buy something, you have made 250 sales, at a conversion cost of $120 per sale.

If the site has multiple conversions, calculating this metric could be difficult because it requires spreading the cost to cover them all.

The cost of accelerating conversion rates online is substantially lower than that incurred in offline channels, because it is cheaper to educate a customer online. With provision of the right online aids, customers can perform product or service research themselves, without costly human interaction.

Unit value of conversion

The *unit value of conversion* can be calculated by dividing the total value of conversions by the number of conversions.

To continue the example given on page 66, the total margin on the 250 sales could be $40 000, giving a unit value of $160 per conversion.

As previously noted (page 64), the value of conversion is not always expressed in financial terms, and this makes the unit value calculations complex. You need to assess how important a conversion is in the overall context of your website before you decide whether to assign this metric. You might then choose to figure out a way of calculating the value of this conversion. For example, let us consider an example in which you distribute a monthly newsletter from a free information portal, and you accept sponsorship or advertisements for each edition. You can calculate the value of each newsletter subscription by dividing the advertising revenue by the subscription base, and then multiplying it by the average length of subscription.

The intrinsic complexities in calculating the value of a conversion to your site might create a lot of work and might cost your organisation more money than the total value of conversions. It is important to be practical. If possible, perform a quick cost/benefit analysis, comparing the cost of collecting and analysing the information with the potential benefits that might come from understanding this information.

Net value of conversion

The *net value of conversion* is a derived metric, calculated by deducting the cost of conversion from the value of conversion. The net value shows whether or not you are making money from the conversion. In other words, it shows the profitability of the conversion. In the campaign example introduced above (pages 66 and 67), the campaign would return $40 profit per conversion from a unit value of $160 and a unit cost of $120. This shows a 33 per cent return on investment.

Conversion metrics can be interrelated and/or multi-tiered. Understanding the relationships between conversion metrics provides a better perspective of net value analysis. For example, an organisation might use an online newsletter purely for its impact on customer retention. Although it is important to track the subscriptions to the newsletter—because these can be considered conversions—and its impact on generating repeat purchases, it might be difficult to attach a value to the newsletter alone. In this case, the value of the newsletter should be analysed from its influence on the purchases—which is another type of conversion.

Number of visits before conversion

Depending on the type of product or service provided, several visits might be required before a customer is fully converted. If a customer is making many visits, your website must answer the various questions that he or she has about what you can offer, and the website must reinforce the notion that the customer is making the right decision. It is important to tie these visits together, not only to ensure that multiple visits lead to conversion, but also to get an insight into how the customers make decisions.

Number of clicks before conversion

As the term suggests, the *number of clicks before conversion* is the average number of clicks required before the conversion process takes place. You can count the exact number of clicks required to make a purchase, starting from your homepage. But customers don't know your site as well as you do, and are therefore likely to make mistakes. Counting up the actual number of clicks-to-purchase (technically known as the *first-purchase momentum*), and comparing this with the minimum number of clicks required to buy something, gives you valuable information about the clarity of your navigation and the online behaviours of the customers. Reducing the first-purchase momentum will increase sales.

Average total time spent before conversion

It is in any organisation's interest to convert users quickly. Faster conversion times indicate a number of positive attributes—the smoothness of the process leading to conversion, how well the audience was targeted, and the closeness of the match between the promise and the presentation of the website. Measuring the average time spent, in conjunction with path to conversion, can help in:

- spotting the users who are having problems (and offering them more assurance and alternative means during the conversion); and
- exploring techniques to speed up the conversion.

The average time for conversion often shows how easily your customers are interacting with you. This figure often correlates with conversion rates. This metric is similar to the previous metric, and reveals the clarity of the site navigation and the online behaviours of customers. Should the website establish behaviour profiles for customer segments, multi-dimensional analysis might be of assistance in understanding the breakdown of the average times of different users. This potentially leads to the design of alternative paths to conversion for different online customer-behaviour groups. A good real-life example of this is the one-click shopping functionality offered by Amazon to the people who seek speedy transactions on its website.

Ratio of upstream conversions for multi-tier conversions

Multi-tier conversion techniques are widespread. Such techniques are in operation when a customer uses a service or product, likes it, becomes dependent on it and, over time, wants to upgrade to a bigger (or better) version. Freeware solutions and services rely on this technique to make money. There are many examples—such as the consolidated search engine called 'copernic.com', webpage download-performance reports from internetseer.com, free website-traffic analysis from hitbox.com, and a free news feed from moreover.com.

A variation on these multi-tier conversions involves the offering of a basic service for free, and then charging for the service once a certain threshold has been reached. Examples of these include yahoo mail, free web-hosting companies, and hosted website-traffic analysis services.

Although there are many reasons for organisations adopting multi-tier conversion, the principle is based upon building brand, satisfaction, and trust. Such techniques can be seen simply as pricing strategies but, to sustain your business, there must be a way of subsidising these products and services. Measuring the ratio of upstream conversions reveals the success of multi-tiering, because it shows the proportion of customers who upgrade their products to the next tier.

Online-affected offline conversions

Analysts predict that total web-impacted spending will exceed US$830 billion by 2005.[1] To measure this, organisations should integrate online and offline channels closely—to capture travel from one channel to another. Understanding the effect of online channels on their offline counterparts is essential to your overall assessment of the success of the online initiatives. This subject is discussed in detail in Chapter 3 (page 26).

Of course, the opposite applies—whereby the offline channels can affect (or facilitate) conversions on the online channels. Therefore, influences from offline channels should also be measured, thus giving the organisation the knowledge it requires to facilitate the customer's travel between channels.

THE RETAIN STAGE METRICS

Having considered the metrics for the *reach* stage (page 54), the *acquire* stage (page 58), and the *convert* stage (page 63), we now turn to the *retain* stage metrics.

Many studies have shown that the cost of retaining customers is much less than the cost of acquiring new ones. This is regardless of the channels used by the business. A McKinsey & Co. study proves that customer retention should be the focus of companies that are seeking profitability and, therefore, returns on their investments. The study shows that improving customer retention—by decreasing abandonment and attrition—is much more valuable to the organisation than other cost-reduction opportunities.[2] See Table 4.1, opposite.

Since this study and similar ones, there has been an increased emphasis on retention. Businesses are shifting the focus from trying to attract as many customers as possible to figuring out better ways to retain their existing high-value customers. The *best customer analysis* (page 80) offers a technique for identifying high-value customers, and for devising strategies to retain them through more targeted and personalised relationship-building activities.

As with conversion, retention has different meanings for different websites. Most websites want customers to come back and perform the desired conversions again and again. For example, if your site is selling CDs, you want your

Table 4.1 Impact of retention on profitability

Impact of a 10 per cent improvement in indicator on current value of e-commerce firms

Metric	Definition	Value	If improved by 10 per cent to	Increase in company value
Attraction				
Visitor acquisition cost	Marketing dollars spent per visitor	$5.68	$5.11	0.7%
New-visitor momentum	Increase in number of new visitors in 2Q vs 1Q	62.4%	68.6%	3.1%
Conversion				
New-customer acquisition cost	Marketing dollars spent per customer	$250	$225	0.8%
New-customer conversion rate	Percentage of new visitors who become customers	4.7%	5.2%	2.3%
New-customer revenue momentum	Increase in new-customer revenue, 2Q vs 1Q	88.5%	97.4%	4.6%
Retention				
Repeat-customer maintenance cost	Operating expenses (less marketing) spent per repeat customer	$1931	$1738	0.7%
Repeat-customer revenue momentum	Increase in revenue from repeat customers, 2Q vs 1Q	21.0%	23.1%	5.8%
Repeat-customer conversion rate	Percentage of customers who become repeat customers	30.2%	33.2%	9.5%
Customer churn rate	Percentage of customers not repeating in first half of 1999	55.3%	49.8%	6.7%

Based on analysis of first-half 1999 data

Source: McKinsey & Company, copyright 2000.

customers to return as many times as possible to buy your CDs. If you are operating a free information portal, you want your customers to return to your site as often as possible, stay there for extensive periods, try new products as they are launched, be exposed to advertising material, and eventually subscribe to a pay service.

However, for certain sites (or components of sites), retention does not indicate success. For example, if your company has a customer-service site that is extremely busy, retention is not necessarily a good indicator. This could simply mean that customers are having problems with your products or services.

Trust is an important factor in retention, because it encourages your customers to come back to your website when they need your products and services. Trust is established through the experiences of customers in their interactions with *all* aspects of your business, not just through experiences with your website. Trust also comes from their experiences of the delivery process and the quality of your goods and services. A consistently good experience will result in a stable and loyal customer base.

Retaining customers is a step in the right direction towards creating loyal customers. However, there is no direct and automatic correlation between retaining a customer and having a loyal customer. People buy books from amazon.com, but this does not mean that they don't buy books from other online or physical retailers. Such customers are *retained* customers for amazon.com, but they are not *loyal* customers. Loyalty implies absoluteness. Loyal customers show absolute attachment to the product, service, brand, or organisation to which they are loyal. Such customers often surpass the traditional customer role, and seek opportunities to promote their loyalties to their families, friends, and acquaintances.

Concepts of retention and loyalty are not new. Many airlines, credit card companies, and retailers have well-established loyalty programs that reward repeat business.

There are strong correlations among the concepts of trust, loyalty, and retention. Customers need to trust your operational processes, your company, and your brands if you are to retain those customers. Research conducted in August 2000

CASE STUDY
Pandora's Online Grocery
Establishing trust through quality products

Pandora's Online Grocery always selects quality fruit and vegetables for its customers. The bananas are always ripe and the tomatoes are firm and red. Customers have sometimes visited one of Pandora's bricks-and-mortar supermarkets and have been surprised to discover that Pandora doesn't always have the same quality produce in its retail outlets, even though the prices seem comparable.

In the physical outlet, choosing the freshest produce is the responsibility of the customers themselves, and the customers have no one to blame if they purchase poor quality produce, rather than the better quality produce that is also available. However, when they order online, they are not granted this opportunity to choose for themselves.

Pandora's online outlet has established trust with its customers by always choosing quality produce for them when they make an online order. Pandora's customers have no hesitation in placing orders—even for items that they have not purchased previously.

by InterTrust of 102 high-profile websites reveals that the most trusted brands are also the best-known brands.[3]

The metrics used to measure the success of the retain stage include:

- the recency of conversion;
- the duration of retention;
- the frequency of retention;
- the value of the customer;
- the cost of retaining the customer;
- the net value of retaining the customer; and
- the percentage share of the customer's business.

Each of these is considered over the page.

CASE STUDY
Stinger's Online Cars
Retention is a step towards loyalty

Stinger's Online Cars cannot expect a particular customer to purchase another car for a long time. If the buying of a new car is how Stinger measures retention, the firm faces a long retention period. But it can do other things to increase customer loyalty to its brand.

For example, Stinger could create an area on its website for a customer's new car. It might contain the specifications of the customer's car, clearly indicating available upgrade options. This would help Stinger to sell accessories to its customer.

It might also include the customer's personal contact details, which the customer could alter if there are any changes. This would increase the accuracy of Stinger's records and give the firm a better chance of contacting the same customer in future.

If the car is financed, Stinger's Online Cars could include this information too. This would save the customer time when seeking information—for taxation purposes, for example.

The car's service records could be entered in the same area. Stinger could automatically send an email alert when the car is due for a service, thus saving the customer the trouble of remembering. Having received the email reminder, the customer could go to the website and make a booking for the service. Alternatively, if the customer wanted to sell the car, this facility would provide easy access to the vehicle's service records.

All of these functions would keep customers coming back to the site, and would create a better experience for them in their interactions with Stinger's Online Cars. Such functions also have the potential to create other types of conversions. If the customers have been happy with their experiences, they are much more likely to consider upgrading their cars with new ones from Stinger's online outlet.

Recency of conversion

Recency of conversion represents the time-lag since the customer's last conversion occurred. Obviously, this time will differ from one site to another, subject to the product or service on offer. For example, if you are selling cars, you would not expect another sales conversion from a customer for at least three years.

Let us assume that you are selling products and services that are purchased frequently. There are two key questions to pose:

■ When do you consider the customer to be retained?
■ How do you influence the process?

Many companies consider that a customer is retained if the customer returns to the website, within a specified time, to conduct various activities. This might be a short time (such as weekly grocery purchases), or it might be a number of years (as with a car purchase). These companies then focus their efforts only on retaining the customers who fall into the recency period, doing nothing to encourage other customers to their site.

Although the principles behind these decisions make sense, the practices that some companies follow are susceptible to error. For example, a customer might buy a product from your website, and then come back within a week to buy another product. After the second purchase, that customer might never return. However, because this customer falls into the definition of retention given above (a customer who has returned within a certain specified time), your company might invest resources in attempting to retain this customer even though this person has no intention of further purchases. In contrast, another customer who comes back at irregular intervals to make purchases might not be considered as 'retained'. Do you cut this second customer off from marketing as soon as one of the purchase intervals falls outside the retention time? Do you stop spending any resources on this customer? The answer to both of these questions should be 'no'.

So you need to be careful about how you define the expected recency period. Should certain segments of your target audience be treated as having different recency periods? What factors influence this? Your accumulated knowledge of your customer base should help you answer these questions.

Duration of retention

The *duration of retention* is the duration between the first and last conversions, and represents how long the customer has been transacting or interacting with the business. A longer duration of retention translates into more loyalty for your business.

Another aspect of this metric is the duration of a customer's visits to the website—which clearly highlights this customer's changing interest. For example, a customer might have been visiting your website on a weekly basis, spending an average of ten minutes on each visit. If this customer's subsequent visits then become significantly longer, this indicates a change in the relationship. It might mean that the customer has new needs that he or she is expecting to fulfil at the website. Alternatively, if the same customer begins to spend less time on the site, it might indicate a diminishing interest in what the website can offer to satisfy that person's needs.

Various companies differ in the emphasis that they place on the duration of visits—in line with the differing objectives of their websites.

Frequency of retention

The *frequency of retention* represents how often the customer performs a particular conversion. It might show how many times the customer has placed orders in a month, or simply how many times that particular customer has visited the site. Frequent purchasers are more likely to continue purchasing.

Like *recency* (see page 75), *frequency* means different things to different sites. A user who purchases groceries from an online grocery on a weekly basis might be considered a loyal customer. Customers who purchase less frequently (perhaps once a month or so) can be enticed to the site more frequently with special promotions or offers. However, it is difficult to entice the loyal weekly shopper to return more frequently.

Frequency of visits to a site that sells expensive items (such as cars or computers) might indicate consideration of purchase. If you can detect an increase in the frequency of visits of certain people, you can take a proactive approach to increase the chances of conversion. For example, a car dealer might dynamically alter the site to promote a test drive, or might start an email campaign to encourage a purchase.

For websites that are designed to enhance business-to-business relationships or to perform business transactions, the frequency of visits acts like the 'pulse' of the relationship. Rapid changes might indicate some form of dissatisfaction, or a profound change in the business relationship. You can use this indicator to act promptly and consult with the customer about the perceived changes in the relationship.

Value of the customer

The *value of the customer* is the total value of the conversions made by a particular customer, and is simply the addition of all individual conversions. Refer to the unit value per conversion metric, previously discussed, for more information on this. (See page 67.)

Best customer analysis techniques (discussed on page 80) illustrate how the monetary value of a customer can be used in developing retention activities, and in estimating the probable value of their future transactions.

Cost of retaining the customer

The *cost of retaining the customer* is the cost of all activities performed to retain a customer, and is therefore known as the *customer-maintenance cost*. The assessment of customer-maintenance costs by channels, together with customer-profitability information, is essential for optimising the amount spent per customer and per order in each channel.

Net value of retaining the customer

The *net value of retaining the customer* is the difference between the forecasted value of a customer's repeat conversions or purchases and the cost of facilitating the purchases. *Best customer analysis* technique (discussed on page 80) suggests a regression method to forecast the value of future purchases based on historical data of recency, frequency, and monetary value. Obviously, negative net values would reveal problems with channel optimisation.

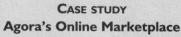

CASE STUDY
Agora's Online Marketplace
Detecting changes in relationship from frequency of online activities

The frequency of activities on Agora's Online Marketplace is the 'pulse' of the relationship with the firm's participating sellers and buyers. Agora can regularly monitor the activity levels of the participants to detect changes.

Agora has a buyer who, over an extended time, has usually procured stationery and computer supplies on a monthly basis. If this buyer does not procure anything for a month, this might mean that this buyer has found another supplier. It might be appropriate for Agora's customer service person to contact the buyer to ascertain the reasons for this change and whether there is any dissatisfaction with the service.

Agora also has a business relationship with the seller of such goods. If this seller stops responding to requests for quotations, and does not update its profile information and product catalogue over an extended time, this might indicate a change in Agora's relationship with the seller. Agora can contact the seller to ascertain the reasons for this change. Agora can then take measures to keep the seller's activity on its marketplace by increasing the relevance and usefulness of its online marketplace to this seller.

Percentage share of the customer's business

The *percentage share of the customer's business* shows the depth of retention, and is a measure of loyalty. It is an important indicator, because your customers might be simultaneously retained by your competitors. Many businesses and individuals deal with multiple vendors at any given time. Two striking examples are the software marketplace and the purchasing of books online.

Many software vendors claim that they 'own' and 'retain' clients, while their competitors simultaneously claim to 'own' and 'retain' the very same clients. Each vendor can produce case studies on these clients, and each can demonstrate the success of its software implementations in serving these clients. Major telecommunications and utility companies, airlines, and multi-nationals always make such lists of 'owned' and 'retained' customers, primarily because different parts of these customer companies use different products from competing vendors. Thus each vendor can truly make the claim that it is 'retaining' these clients.

In the case of online book purchasing, some people regularly buy from amazon.com. But this doesn't prevent these customers buying books from other online and offline bookstores. Book-purchasing involves impulsive behaviour—if a person comes across an interesting book, that person buys it on the spot. The customer doesn't necessarily wait until he or she is online to buy the book from amazon.com. Rather, if the book is noticed when the customer passes a bookshop on the street, the purchase is made then and there.

But not all book purchases are impulsive. Customers might shop at amazon.com when they need to research a particular subject. The site's excellent functionality shows them an entire list of the books in a particular category, thus allowing for easy comparison. Customers can also read the reviews and ratings given by other users, and can look at other books these people have read. This helps the customers make rational decisions on their purchases. In a physical bookshop, it is difficult for customers to learn about other books and other people's opinions. Interaction with other buyers is limited, and the cataloguing is much poorer—with the choice often being limited by the decisions of the category manager.

All in all, amazon.com knows that it is retaining particular customers. However, the local bookshop thinks the same, because its customers chat to the shopkeeper every time they visit the shop.

As a website operator, the important thing is to look beyond the fact that you are retaining a customer, and to analyse *how much* of that customer's business you are retaining. This is *the percentage share of the customer's business*. It is not an easy figure to calculate, but you can follow different techniques to estimate your share. If amazon.com asked its customers about their annual spending on books, their customers would probably tell them. But they haven't asked yet!

In contrast, many software companies do try to gather this information. However, unfortunately, they tend to get their timing wrong. They often ask their customers about their annual spending on IT while their customers are researching new software (that is, in the *acquisition* or *conversion* stages). Instead, these software vendors should pose the question once they have successfully retained the customers, when they are more inclined to give an accurate answer.

BEST CUSTOMER ANALYSIS

The database marketing concept of recency, frequency, and monetary (RFM) value analysis applies well to websites that contain conversion expressed in monetary value. This will be referred to as *best customer analysis*.

When to use

Best customer analysis has two primary functions:

■ segmenting the customers; and
■ predicting future value of conversions.

Customer segmentation enables you to devise more suitable strategies to engage with customers. You can create segments in areas such as marketing, sales, and customer service—balancing the value of a segment against the cost of engaging with that segment. Customer segmentation also helps you to understand the profile of the target market, based on the characteristics of the customers in the segment, so you can then reach more targeted market segments.

Because it is based on historical interactions with customers, this technique makes it possible to predict the likely outcomes of future interactions. This is an important exercise because it can be used to optimise the net value of these interactions.

How to use

Best customer analysis requires three data elements, all of which were introduced as metrics for the *retain* stage earlier in this chapter (see page 70).

These are:

■ recency;
■ frequency; and
■ monetary value.

Each of these is now considered in the context of best customer analysis.

Recency
Recency shows whether the customer has made a purchase or visited your site recently. Statistical analysis shows that customers who have made a purchase recently are more likely to purchase again in the near future. The nature of the product sold on your website will determine the length of the recency period— the number of years since the purchase of a new car, the number of weeks since the purchase of groceries, or the number of days since visiting a news portal.

Frequency
Frequency shows how many times the customer has entered the *conversion* phase on your site, whether it be to place an order or simply to visit. Frequent purchasers are more likely to repeat their purchasing in future. The frequency of purchases or visits acts like the 'pulse' of the relationship with the customer, with rapid changes indicating variations in the relationship.

Monetary value
The *monetary value* shows the total value of the purchases made by the customer. You can start measuring actual monetary value only after the customer has made an initial purchase. From this point on, the customer's future value and profitability can be measured. This data element is applicable only to websites that are able to attach monetary value to conversions. For websites that primarily influence offline sales, you can consider the monetary value from the offline sales in the analysis.

Segmenting the customers
To segment the customers, each one of the above data elements (recency, frequency, and monetary value) is ranked separately in ascending order and assigned into quintiles. For example, all customers are ranked by the frequency of their purchases, sorted in an ascending order. Then the first 20 per cent are assigned to quintile one, the second 20 per cent to quintile two, and so forth. A three-dimensional representation of the final outcome is depicted in Figure 4.1 (page 83).

As can be seen in Figure 4.1, the customers with the lowest values of recency, frequency, and monetary value are assigned to the RFM cell 111. This cell represents the customers with the least value to your organisation. Conversely, RFM cell 555 indicates the customers with highest values of these data elements.

Each cell of the RFM customer-segmentation cube provides a unique insight into your customers' purchasing or interaction behaviours. You can use this information to treat your customers in a more strategic way.

Predicting future values

Using the same data elements, the value of next conversion can be predicted. In his book titled *Database Marketing: The Ultimate Tool*, Edward Nash provides a regression analysis equation for forecasting a customer's next order size.[4] It reads as follows:

next order size = average order size + (recency coefficient x recency)
+ (frequency coefficient x frequency)

The coefficients are calculated by regression analysis techniques, based on the historical data.

Let us apply this formula to our fictitious online grocery store, Pandora's Online Grocery, using a number of examples. Based on statistical analysis of historical data, it might be shown that a particular customer's order size will be $10 lower for each week that has passed since the last order, and $5 higher for each additional purchase. Then the equation to predict the next order size will be:

next order size = average order size + (−10 x recency) + (+5 x frequency)

Let us now consider two customers:

Customer 1

So far, this customer's average order size at Pandora's Online Grocery has been $100. The customer's last visit was within the last week, and so far the customer has made ten purchases.

next order size = $100 + (−10 x 1) + (+5 x 10) = $140

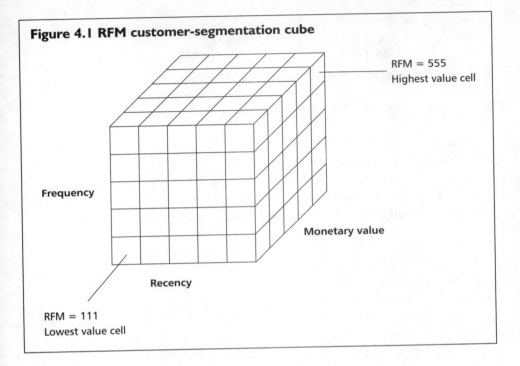

Figure 4.1 RFM customer-segmentation cube

RFM = 555
Highest value cell

Frequency

Monetary value

Recency

RFM = 111
Lowest value cell

Customer 2

This customer has also spent $100 (average order), but has bought groceries only once, ten weeks ago.

$$\text{next order size} = \$100 + (-10 \times 10) + (+5 \times 1) = \$5$$

The results show that the expected size of order for the second customer is substantially lower than for the first customer. The cost of trying to reinitiate the second customer could be an expensive task, and might not be profitable.

CUSTOMER-ENGAGEMENT FUNNEL

The *customer-engagement funnel* is a powerful tool with which to visualise the overall engagement performance with customers.

When to use

This analysis technique has three primary functions:

■ to consolidate certain engagement metric results;
■ to identify the bottlenecks from a high-level overview; and
■ to forecast high level customer activities in the future.

How to use

See Figure 4.2 (opposite). In an ideal world, you might expect the funnel to be the same width as we move from one phase in the engagement process to the next. In other words, the size of audience that has been reached should equal the size of the audience that is retained. Unfortunately, this is rarely the case.

The shape of the customer-engagement funnel is influenced by a number of factors, including the purpose of your website, the composition of your target audience, your operational strategies, and their execution. If you are reaching consumers with your website, the funnel usually narrows rapidly. If you are reaching business partners—with whom you have established relationships—the shape of the funnel might remain more uniform. There are also websites for which the retain cycle is not an issue. In this case, the organisation would not want to retain the visitors—because the organisation is concerned only with a single event of short lifespan, or because the organisation requires a visitor to participate only once (such as voting at a national election). These various situations are depicted in Figure 4.2 (opposite).

The effectiveness of the engagement stages determines the shape of the funnel. To achieve the optimum (uniform) funnel shape, organisations should strive for better targeted *reach*, well-designed *acquisition* functionality, a good experience during the *convert* stage, and suitable *retention* activities.

The customer-engagement funnel, when expressed in different units of measure, can reveal insightful information. You can draw funnels for the total value of customers, the total cost of maintaining customers, and the net value of customers. These will show where your resources are invested and where the opportunities exist for further engagement with your customers. It also provides a tool for setting target values.

Figure 4.2 Funnel shapes for different websites

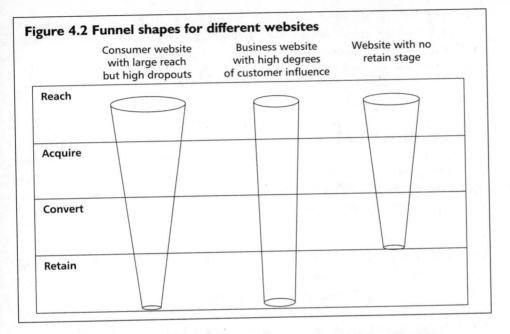

Consumer website with large reach but high dropouts

Business website with high degrees of customer influence

Website with no retain stage

Reach

Acquire

Convert

Retain

INTERNET TRAFFIC MEASUREMENT AND RANKING

Internet traffic-measurement companies provide various services about overall Internet traffic volumes. They can drill down to the distribution of Internet traffic to particular websites, including overall and industry-specific site rankings, and comparative traffic analysis with similar sites.

When to use

This analysis technique has two primary functions:

▪ explaining changes in traffic volumes; and
▪ gathering competitive intelligence.

When changes in traffic volumes cannot be explained by analysing internal factors, reports from external Internet traffic-measurement companies become extremely valuable. These reports help you understand external factors—such as a competitor's marketing push, or major holidays and sporting events—and their impact on your business.

Some of these companies can provide comparative analysis with competitive and similar sites. You can request that they measure your competitors' websites and provide a comparison of basic metrics—such as the number of unique sessions, page-views, and visit durations—in a given period of time.

How to use

The providers of these services often measure basic metrics such as unique sessions, page-views, and visit durations. There are many players in this market segment, but there is no standard methodology for how they collect, cleanse, aggregate, and extrapolate their results. Their results therefore vary. Understanding the various methodologies on the market can help you select the right service provider. This knowledge will also help you interpret their results more meaningfully.

It is important to be aware that none of these firms can measure the entire Internet traffic. They measure only a sample of base data, from which they extrapolate overall web usage and website rankings.

Some will measure from a panel of users by installing tracking software on their computers. This software records the panel members' surfing patterns and sends these to the measurement company. The biggest criticism faced by these service providers is concern with the scope of their data collection. For example, the measurement service with the biggest panel size has a panel of 220 000 people worldwide, 70 000 of whom are resident in the United States of America.

Another category of these measurement firms gets its raw data from the caches collected at the proxy servers of ISPs. However, these data are biased by the relationship between the measurement vendor and the ISP, and by the subscriber demographics of the ISP. In countries where the ISP market is dominated by a small number of players—and where a single service provider can therefore measure the bulk of the traffic—the accuracy of the result increases significantly.

Yet another category produces base data by aggregating from hosted site-centric website analysis services provided to their clients (with the clients' permission).

There are also others that combine multiple techniques—such as a combination of panel and site-centric data.

The target audience of your website should be a primary factor when choosing the right measurement vendor for that website, because the Internet access method and geographical location of the measurement vendor will determine which category of vendor fits best. Websites that attract significant traffic from overseas countries might be penalised by both panel-based and proxy server-based data-collection techniques. These data sources are often specific to a single country. In addition, users with broadband Internet access are not included in usage data collected from proxy servers.

Moreover, panel members are often home users, because few companies would allow externally owned and controlled tracking software to be installed on their corporate networks. As a result, site visits conducted at a workplace are often underreported.

Finally, the methodologies employed by these service providers require traditional web browsers. As more and more users access the Internet through Internet devices, an increasing amount of traffic will be excluded from the data.

With so many methodologies and influencing factors, it is no wonder that each vendor produces different results. However, it shouldn't stop you from using these services. Their reports offer valuable insights into web traffic.

Visit <www.hurolinan.com> to read the reviews of *Internet traffic-measurement service providers* [Locator Code 101].

WHERE FROM—TO ANALYSIS

Where from—to analysis reveals how traffic arrives at a website, indicating which website your customer visited immediately before he or she arrived at your site, and which site your customer goes to immediately after leaving your site.

When to use

This technique can be used:

▋ to gauge the effectiveness of the reach techniques (such as affiliate networks, search engine registrations, and online promotions of banner advertisements and sponsorship buttons), and to obtain additional information about site visitors and their interests; and

▋ to understand customer movements to spot shoppers in the competitive marketplace.

How to use

This analysis can be conducted in a very limited capacity from website-traffic analysis. Because the web is stateless, such analysis can capture only the *referrer* information, which is derived from data collected when a person clicks on a link provided on another site, and that person consequently arrives at your site. Thereafter, website-traffic analysis cannot identify the website that is visited by the same user immediately *after* leaving your site.

When users enter a website after being referred from another site, the server log files can capture the details of the referring website and can store them in a data element called a 'referrer tag'. For search engine referrals, in addition to the name of the search engine, log files can also capture the keywords that have been used to locate the site in the search engine.

Websites that rely heavily on referral traffic from other sites employ more sophisticated methods for capturing referral information. The affiliate sites of amazon.com provide a good example. When users click on a link to a book from one of these sites, they are taken directly to the page that displays the book on the Amazon site. The URL of the Amazon page contains the referral source and the book identifier.

Some Internet users might have also noticed that when they click on a link from an email newsletter, the link opens a webpage with additional numbers appended to the URL of the page. These numbers tell the operator of the website that the user has arrived from the email newsletter.

It is important to understand the limitations of these techniques, which are listed below.

■ Research conducted by Internet Advertising Bureau (IAB) Market Poll shows that '55 per cent of users remember or write down the company and product and check it out later'.[5] Relying on referrer tags alone to measure the effectiveness of online promotional reach techniques can therefore be incorrect—because such techniques discount the majority of customers who do not immediately follow referral links.
■ If page content is dynamically served from a database or is sourced externally, search engines will not be able to index the content of the page. If search engine referrals are the key to generating traffic to your site, you will need to rely on metatags for indexing pages. (For more detailed discussions on search engine registration and defining effective metatags, readers are recommended to refer to the books on this subject.)
■ There might be other opportunities to ask customers directly how they have found the site. These include registration or online polls.

Organisations that are seriously interested in this technique should procure these services from an external provider. These vendors are able to provide a richer array of information, and can capably address many of the issues outlined above, as they do not rely only on referral information. They can capture the details of where a user has been immediately before and after visiting your site. The principles of how they capture these data is similar to those for Internet traffic-measurement and ranking (see page 85). It is important to understand their methodologies before engaging a service provider.

Visit <www.hurolinan.com> to read the reviews of *where from—to analysis service providers* [Locator Code 102].

SUMMARY

Every aspect of the *customer-centric measurement framework* (as outlined in Figure 2.1, page 16, and developed in subsequent chapters) is measurable. The present chapter has outlined the metrics and analysis techniques for each customer-engagement stage. Because each site is unique, specific metrics are required for each site to measure success. The metrics provided in this section are generic, but provide a guide to defining metrics for your website.

Calculating the results of metrics is sufficient in many instances, because it does indicate how performance expectations are being met. To explain the results further, however, one must perform analysis. Four analysis techniques have been discussed in this chapter:

▮ *best customer analysis*—to segment customers and predict future values of conversions;
▮ the *customer-engagement funnel*—to consolidate engagement metric results, identify the bottlenecks from a high-level overview, and to forcast high level customer activities in the future;
▮ Internet *measurement and ranking services*—to explain the effect of changes in traffic volumes, and to gather competitive intelligence; and
▮ *where from—to analysis*—to gauge effectiveness of the reach techniques, and to understand customer movements in the competitive marketplace.

CHAPTER

5

Explaining Dropouts

It is obvious that the *reach* stage represents a website's potential whereas the *convert* and *retain* stages affect bottom-line results for the business. As discussed in the previous chapters, there will be dropouts when moving from one stage to another.

Understanding the numbers and patterns of dropouts is as valuable, if not more so, than understanding the successes. Therefore, organisations should track dropouts and learn more about why they occur. This acquired information will help you make changes to your website and adjust operational strategies to contain these dropouts.

This chapter discusses the different types of dropouts, provides generic metrics, and introduces the technique of *multi-dimensional analysis*.

LEAKAGE

Leakage occurs when you persuade people to visit your website, but these people leave without entering into the *convert* stage. Major causes of leakage are:

▌ a mismatch between the promise given by the *reach* technique and the capabilities of the website;
▌ ineffectiveness of the reach technique to attract the targeted audience; and
▌ poor functionality for guiding and encouraging the user to enter the *convert* stage.

Leakages from the entry pages to a website are usually the biggest issue for many sites, because a large proportion of users visit an entry page but then leave without exploring the site further. The entry page is not necessarily the homepage, because reach techniques such as search engine registrations sometimes link to a deeper page in the site.

Measuring the leakage levels and analysing the reasons behind them can help you increase the chances of moving the customers deeper into the engagement process—into the convert stage. Metrics to measure leakages include:

- number of leakages;
- ratio of leakages to acquisitions; and
- opportunity cost of leakage.

Each of these is considered below.

Number of leakages

The *number of leakages* is the number of people who visit the website but do not enter into the convert stage. It is important to remember that some conversions require multiple visits to a website, in which case you must give them a few chances before considering them to be a leakage. This requires distinguishing first-time visitors from repeat visitors, through a user-identification technique such as cookies. For example, if a user has visited Stinger's Online Cars a number of times without going into any of the conversion processes, but has not returned to the site for more than two weeks, Stinger can assume that this person has been leaked.

Ratio of leakages to acquisitions

As the term suggests, the *ratio of leakages to acquisitions* is the ratio of the number of leakages to the number of acquisitions. This metric shows the effectiveness of the *acquisition* functionality and the *reach* techniques in bringing targeted users to the site.

Opportunity cost of leakage

The *opportunity cost of leakage* shows the financial impact of the missed opportunity, in terms of lost revenue. It can be calculated by multiplying the number of leakages by an estimated conversion value.

If more information is known about the visitor leaking from the site, a more accurate estimate of the opportunity cost is possible. For example, a particular person might enter your site from one that typically attracts high-value customers—as identified by *best customer analysis* (see page 80). The opportunity cost of this leakage can be considered greater than for someone entering via another technique, such as a search engine.

CASE STUDY
Vault's Information Portal
Containing leakage by path analysis

Vault's Information Portal contains a directory service whereby only registered users can search service providers of some type. The service providers directory includes detailed reviews and ratings, not merely names and addresses. Because Vault's portal invests significant resources to maintain the directory, and because the customer attaches a significant value to this service, Vault can decide to offer this service, although it is free, to registered users only.

After examining the paths that cause leakage, Vault might establish that the user-registration process is causing significant leakages from the site. The visitors intend to search the directory but leave the site without registering. To contain the leakages and encourage users to register, Vault has two options—remove the registration process or enhance the features that demonstrate the value of the directory services.

Vault decides to take the second option because the first would impede its ability to identify users and to understand their needs in any detail. Vault therefore designs a feature that allows visitors to search the directory *without* registering, but that displays search results in only a summary format. Those visitors who want to read detailed reviews and ratings of a service provider still need to register.

Subsequently, Vault's portal receives an increase in the page-views and, more importantly, an increase in the number of registered users and a decrease in leakage.

To understand the causes of leakages fully, and to work to contain them, the operators of websites can perform *path analysis* and/or *multi-dimensional analysis*.

Path analysis (see Chapter 6, page 122) entails a detailed examination of all the activities that a user performs before leaving the site. Knowledge of the leakage path can assist in redesigning the content and making certain messages crisper.

Multi-dimensional analysis (discussed, below, on page 101) provides insight

---

CASE STUDY
Vault's Information Portal
Containing leakage by multi-dimensional analysis

Vault's Information Portal can use many reach techniques, including referrals from corporate intranets. By examining the ratio of leakages to acquisitions, Vault might identify that the ratio is minimal when users are referred from corporate intranets. These users immediately enter the *convert* stage, registering to use the service.

With this knowledge, Vault can start a marketing campaign to corporations that might benefit from the services of his information portal, encouraging them to list the portal in their intranets. By doing this, Vault will decrease the number of leakages and its ratio to acquisitions.

---

into the composition of leakages by drilling into information such as reach techniques, and entry and exit pages. The result of this analysis reveals the areas that the operators of the websites should focus on.

ABANDONMENT

Having considered *leakage* (page 92), we now turn to *abandonment*. Abandonment occurs when a user decides to leave the conversion process half-way through. It differs from leakage in that, for abandonment to occur, the user must have started the *conversion* process.

Any conversion process can lead to abandonments. Shopping-cart abandonment in retailer websites has attracted significant attention because of its clear difference from what happens in the bricks-and-mortar world. It is very rare for a shopper in a bricks-and-mortar supermarket to fill a shopping trolley and then leave it, and all its contents, without going through the checkout line.

Researchers have attempted to estimate the actual online shopping-cart abandonment rate, but there are significant discrepancies in their reports. Andersen Consulting[1] and Forrester Research[2] both show online shopping-cart abandonment rates of 25 per cent. Jupiter Communications[3] reports an abandonment rate of 27 per cent. eMarketer[4] reports 32 per cent as the actual rate, whereas NetEffect[5] and Greenfield Online[6] claim it is 67 per cent.

The reasons for abandonment are more consistent, being cited by researchers as poor site navigation and usability.

High levels of abandonment indicate intrinsic problems for a website, and this is therefore an important issue that warrants a close examination of causes and cure. Metrics to measure abandonment include:

- number of abandonments;
- ratio of abandonments to conversions; and
- cost of abandonment.

Each of these is discussed below.

Number of abandonments

The *number of abandonments* is, as the term suggests, the number of conversions abandoned. For shopping-cart abandonments, the measurement can be performed at two levels—the number of carts abandoned and the number of items abandoned. If the conversion process includes shipment of physical goods, the measure should include the cancellations and returns. This varies from *attrition* (see, below, page 98) because, in this case, the customer places the order and then cancels it before the product is shipped, or returns the product after it has been received.

Jupiter Media Metrix estimates that online retailers will be facing 90 million returned items by 2005, concluding that the best way to cut costs and keep customers happy is to track closely why goods have been returned, and to respond quickly.[7]

Ratio of abandonment to conversions

Again, this term is relatively self-explanatory. The *ratio of abandonment to conversions* is the ratio of the number of abandonments to the number of conversions.

For shopping-cart abandonments, additional metrics can be monitored—such as the ratio of the number of items per abandoned cart to the number of completed transactions.

Cost of abandonment

The *cost of abandonment* is the opportunity cost of lost revenue to the organisation if the abandonment does *not* involve cancellations and returns.

If cancellations and returns *are* involved, the cost calculations could be complex—depending on the fulfilment chain and how the cost is distributed to different parts of the chain. McKinsey Quarterly reports that the value of online retailer returns constitutes 11 per cent of revenue.[8] Jupiter Media Metrix estimates that returned items will amount to US$5.8 billion of merchandise by 2005.[9]

The cost of processing online returns represents a significant percentage of operating expenses. For online retailers trying to make a profit, this is a key metric to watch. Consequently, organisations should track, explain, and identify ways of reducing returns. A 'no-questions-asked' returns policy can impede an organisation's ability to understand why the goods are returned.

Path analysis (see Chapter 6, page 122) can be used to identify and understand all the activities that take place before the user abandons the conversion process. Such analysis helps you to reduce the abandonment rate. This might be achieved by fixing pages that cause problems and, in more sophisticated sites, by personalising the experience or offering real-time help when the system thinks the user is having difficulty. It is important to note that every click added to the persuasion-and-conversion process increases the risk of abandonment.

Multi-dimensional analysis (see this chapter, page 101) can be used to understand trends in individual product categories and customer segments, profiles of shoppers vs buyers, and the profiles of products abandoned vs products purchased. Equipped with this information, you can spot shoppers who demonstrate characteristics of abandonment, and offer them incentives to stay and complete the conversion.

Combining path analysis and multi-dimensional analysis, it might be possible to identify and design suitable paths to conversion that cater better to the online behaviours of different users.

ATTRITION

Having considered *leakage* (page 92) and *abandonment* (page 95), we now turn to *attrition*. Attrition occurs when converted customers cease buying from you, and take their business elsewhere. Examples of attrition include people who have unsubscribed from a newsletter during a specific period of time, those who have switched utility providers from one vendor to another, or those who have changed travel agents or credit cards.

Attrition is the barometer of your business. A high number of attritions is an indicator of poor performance, and therefore needs attention. Even more indicative than the number of attritions is the *attrition rate*, which is the ratio of attrited customers to newly converted customers. A high attrition rate is a clear indication that your company is doing something wrong or that your competition is appealing to your customer base with better products and services.

Attrition is very different from both leakage and abandonment and is, unfortunately, more difficult to address. With attrition, you are dealing with customers who previously perceived you to be a good partner and previously valued your products and services, but who have now decided to leave you. It is akin to a marriage divorce, as opposed to a 'one-night stand'—because the relationship now lost was previously valued. With leakage and abandonment, you had not yet managed to convert these customers.

In services that require regular payments, such as membership fees and utility bills, attrition is more visible and therefore easier to calculate. In these circumstances, customers have to notify you when they are ceasing the service or, alternatively, you can be aware that they have simply not renewed their subscription.

If your products and services do not fall into this easily detectable category, you will need to devise methods for diagnosing attrition. For example, if you are operating an online music store and one of your customers, who previously had a profile of buying a CD every week does not make a purchase for more than a month, this person might have attrited you and gone elsewhere. Similarly, if you sell cars online, and if you have not heard from a particular customer for more than five years, this customer might have bought another brand of car. If you are operating an online flight-booking company, and if a customer stops earning frequent-flyer points at a rate consistent with his or her normal profile, this person might have attrited you and gone to another flight-booking company, or might have undergone a major lifestyle change.

If you are operating membership services, you will usually have an opportunity to ask the customer why he or she is attriting you, and which of your competitors this former member is moving to. In other cases, you might have to put in place techniques to confirm attrited customers and contrive opportunities to convert them back. It might be that the customer no longer requires the service your business offers—because the customer is changing work or moving elsewhere. It is therefore important to determine the reason for attriting.

However, a sudden, large number of attritions is unlikely to be customer-specific, and is more likely to be caused by a generic product or service abandonment—since all your customers will not be leaving the country or getting out of business together. They might be converting to a better product, such as moving from analogue phones to digital. In these circumstances, your company would (it is to be hoped!) already know about this before it happens.

Understanding why attrition happens will help you retain your other existing customers.

As with some of the other dropout metrics, some of the attrition metrics are simply the reverse of retention metrics.

Attrition metrics include:

- number of attritions;
- attrition rate;
- churn rate;
- cost of processing attritions; and
- net value of reconverting.

Each of these is considered below.

Number of attritions
The *number of attritions* is the number of people who have attrited within a period of time. Spotting these and classifying them according to the reasons for their leaving will indicate what you need to focus on to retain your other customers or to reconvert attrited customers.

Attrition rate
The *attrition rate* is the ratio of attrited customers to newly converted customers during a period of time. For instance, if a weekly online newsletter experiences 50 people unsubscribing in a given month, while attracting 100 new subscribers, the attrition rate is 50:100 (that is, 0.5).

Churn rate
Churn is the ratio of attrited customers to *all* customers during a period of time. For instance, if the same newsletter mentioned above had a total of 7000 subscribers at the end of the month, 50 unsubscribing customers during the month would produce a churn rate of 50:7000 (that is, 0.007).

Churn rate is a popular measure with ISPs, but is also applicable to other businesses. The attrition rate, which is very similar, considers *both* attriting and new customers, and is a better indication of growth. The churn rate, on the other hand, considers *only* attritions and can be misleading if not looked at together with the growth rate.

Cost of attrition

The *cost of attrition* is the dollar value of attrition in terms of both lost sales and foregone profit. In addition to the attrition and churn rates, organisations should look at the cost of attrition and compare it with overall financial figures to find out about the growth or reduction in business.

Unit cost of processing attritions

The *unit cost of processing attritions* is the cost associated with spotting attritions and gathering information associated with them—such as the reasons for leaving and the competitors they have chosen to go to. This metric applies because the detection and analysis of attrition can be a complex and expensive process for certain types of businesses.

Net value of reconverting

The *net value of reconverting* is the difference between the future value of retaining an attrited customer and the cost of reconverting this attrited customer. The cost of reconverting attrited customers could be higher than the cost of retaining them, because reconverting is dealing with customers who have chosen to leave your business, and who therefore require persuasion to return.

MULTI-DIMENSIONAL ANALYSIS

Multi-dimensional analysis drills down from an overall metric result to the multiple individual data elements (dimensions) that comprise the result. In other words, it shows the metric results from the point of view of the other data elements.

When to use

The primary use of this technique is to understand the possible underlying causes of the performance by examining its composition from different dimensions. Its value is derived from identifying and understanding relationships among data elements, rather than simply looking at the data elements themselves.

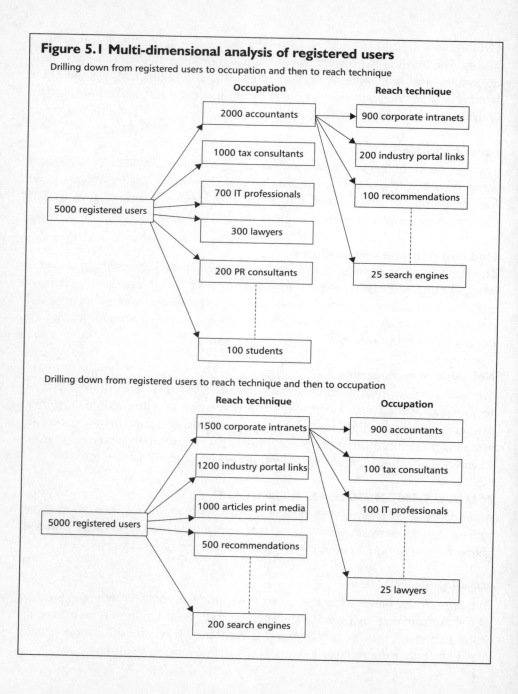

Figure 5.1 Multi-dimensional analysis of registered users

Drilling down from registered users to occupation and then to reach technique

Occupation

Reach technique

5000 registered users

2000 accountants

1000 tax consultants

700 IT professionals

300 lawyers

200 PR consultants

100 students

900 corporate intranets

200 industry portal links

100 recommendations

25 search engines

Drilling down from registered users to reach technique and then to occupation

Reach technique

Occupation

5000 registered users

1500 corporate intranets

1200 industry portal links

1000 articles print media

500 recommendations

200 search engines

900 accountants

100 tax consultants

100 IT professionals

25 lawyers

How to use

This concept applies to virtually all aspects of a website. Taking the number of registered users on a website as an example, multi-dimensional analysis provides various insights into this metric. Let us assume that *occupation* and the *reach technique* are two other data elements collected during the registration process. This makes it possible to examine the relative effectiveness of reach techniques on particular occupations. See Figure 5.1 (opposite).

The first section of Figure 5.1 shows that accountants comprise the bulk of registered users, and half of them have been reached through the links provided in their firms' corporate intranets. The second part of the figure shows that links on corporate intranets work best for accountants. Presuming that accountants are your target audience, armed with this information you can focus on further developing this reach technique to bring more accountants to the site.

Similarly, this technique can be used for other aspects of a website—from the consumption of different content categories to shopping-cart abandonments. The only prerequisite is the ability to relate separate data elements. It is therefore essential to understand how this technique operates so you can identify data elements to capture and build relationships among them.

To perform multi-dimensional analysis proficiently, a technical infrastructure consisting of a data warehouse and an online analytical processing (OLAP) tool is needed.

SUMMARY

Dropouts occur at every stage of the engagement process, and the ability to measure and analyse these dropouts improves service and retains customers. There are several generic metrics and analysis techniques for the three types of dropout—leakage, abandonment, and attrition.

Multi-dimensional analysis is a technique that is used to understand the possible underlying causes of dropouts—by examining the composition from different data dimensions.

CHAPTER

6

Containing Dropouts

What keeps your customers coming back to your website? Frequent updates, high-quality content, fast page downloads, and simple navigation and functionality are the keys to retaining your customers. A poll of 8600 web households conducted by Forrester Research's Media Field Study revealed that users returned to their favourite sites for the strong content (75 per cent) and regular turnover of information (54 per cent). Snappy designs that load quickly (58 per cent) and ease of use (66 per cent) were two other important factors. In contrast, users said that branding (13 per cent), cutting-edge technology (12 per cent), chat, and a bulletin board system (BBS) (10 per cent) had little effect on their decision to return.[1]

Therefore, it is apparent that the major factors influencing dropouts are *content appropriateness*, *design effectiveness*, and *website-performance efficiency*. Metrics can help you measure the impact of dropouts on your business *after* they have occurred (as discussed in Chapter 5). In contrast, the metrics for the factors that *influence* the dropouts are more proactive, because they help you to pinpoint reasons for dropouts *before* they take place. These metrics are the subject of the present chapter.

Many of these influencing factors relate to the *usability* of the site. Research conducted by Jakob Nielson claims that high-traffic sites have better usability metrics.[2] Website usability shows how well a site is geared to the online behaviours of customers in their interactions with the site. *Usability-testing* is introduced in this chapter, along with two other important analytical techniques—*path analysis* and *onsite search-effectiveness analysis*.

CONTENT APPROPRIATENESS

The expectation that they will find the right content is the main reason for people visiting a website. A subsequent positive judgment on the site's content quality and currency is the main reason for their return. The Forrester research quoted above ranks content as the top factor in driving repeat visits to a website—being accountable for 75 per cent of repeat visits.

Content can be delivered in various formats and media. It might contain information about products and services, news releases, reports, or corporate

---

CASE STUDY
Pandora's Online Grocery
Using accumulated knowledge of customers for retention

The ability to create shopping lists from the previous purchases of a particular customer is one of the motivations for that customer to go back to Pandora's Online Grocery. This is a creative way of enhancing retention.

Pandora's Online Grocery keeps records of customers' previous purchases and allows these customers to create different standard shopping lists. This functionality is extremely useful, and it deters customers from using a competitor's site because of the time it would take them to set up their shopping lists again.

This is not about 'tying' customers to Pandora's business. Rather, it is about Pandora's use of accumulated knowledge to offer its customers a more streamlined experience when they come to its website.

---

information; or it might simply consist of pictures, audio, or video. It could be developed interactively and progressively through discussion forums, or it could be a tool that responds to a set of questions to provide a recommendation or quote. It could be comparison of products, based on a standard or user-selected set of criteria.

An organisation's website might contain content that has been created internally, content created collaboratively with the audience, or content sourced from an external organisation. The accumulated knowledge of customers' activities at websites can help to create better content—content that provides more efficient and effective ways of serving customers' interests during repeat visits. That is, you can use the knowledge to work on *retaining* customers.

So it is the *content* that gets the message across and meets the requirements of your users. With this in mind, you should be aware of every content piece on your website, and the role it plays in your users' experiences. Each method of content creation has a different price tag attached to it.

CASE STUDY
Pandora's Online Grocery
Cost trade-off for content creation

Pandora's Online Grocery displays its full online catalogue, irrespective of whether items are currently in stock or not. It would be better if the online catalogue and the warehouse inventory were identical, but Pandora's online system is not fully integrated with its warehouse inventory system. Pandora has investigated this possibility, but has discovered that this is presently cost-prohibitive, and involves complex logistical problems.

Relatively sophisticated customers will be aware that Pandora's online system is not integrated with its warehouse inventory system. For such customers, the implication is that they might be ordering products that they have no guarantee of receiving in a reasonable time. Stock-outs are infrequent, but they might occur when a customer needs a particular ingredient for a dinner party that evening. If that should happen, Pandora's Online Grocery will not save the customer from a much-dreaded supermarket visit, and the customer might even consider shopping elsewhere after such inconvenience.

Pandora's Online Grocery knows this. Because the integration of its retail and warehousing systems is expensive and logistically impractical, Pandora offers the customer an alternative service whereby replacement items are nominated for out-of-stock items—if the customer has agreed, in advance, to accept such replacement products. This information stays on the customer's profile, and the customer can turn it off at any time for a particular transaction.

This is an example of creating the right content in the most cost-effective manner, and it does the job for most customers—as long as they do not receive too many replacement products. And Pandora ensures that they do not!

As a matter of commonsense, your organisation wants to create the right content in the most cost-effective manner. In measuring the effectiveness of your website, you should therefore consider the cost of creating and maintaining content.

Metrics to measure the appropriateness of content include:

- stickiness factor;
- relevance factor;
- freshness factor;
- personalisation index;
- content exposure; and
- impact on competition.

Each of these is discussed below.

Stickiness factor

The *stickiness factor* is the amount of interest that a content piece generates in a user, thus demonstrating the attractiveness and relevance of the content. It is measured by the average time that each person spends on the site.

Measuring the stickiness factor for different content areas, and comparing this with expected values, provides useful information for the operators of websites. For example, if you have a 700-word media release on your site, and you know that the average reading time is three minutes (based on historical data on similar-sized media releases), you can measure the stickiness factor to see if people are reading it. If reading time falls below three minutes, you will know that the media release is less relevant and less appealing to your users.

A more detailed analysis of the stickiness factor should include the use of *multi-dimensional analysis* (Chapter 5, page 101). This links the content piece to the reach techniques used, and compares its consumption against the consumption of other similar material—which is important as the amount of interest generated by a new content piece also relates to how it has been promoted.

Internet *traffic-measurement and ranking* (Chapter 4, page 85) report the stickiness factor for high-traffic websites. You can use these reports to compare the stickiness factor of your website with competitors' sites or similar sites.

Like many other metrics, the stickiness factor should be interpreted with caution. It might very well mean that your site is not as efficient as that of your competitors.

For example, assessing the booking functionalities provided in two travel sites might show that one of them is more efficient than the other because it takes less time to complete a booking. *Usability-testing* (this chapter, page 129) can reveal if this is the case.

Furthermore, a high stickiness factor can indicate poor performance in certain websites, particularly if people are spending a lot of time in the customer service and support pages. It might indicate that people are having problems with your products and are trying to seek solutions. For example, on an information portal, if the stickiness factor for the pages that contain privacy policies or user agreements is significantly higher than for similar pages on other sites, it might indicate that people refer to these pages more than once and have concerns about the portal's policies.

Relevance factor

The *relevance factor* indicates how much of a website is relevant to a user. It can be calculated by dividing the number of content pieces that a user consumes by the number of available content pieces or expected content consumption. For example, on Vault's Information Portal, there might be twenty articles that apply to the profile of the user (that is, they should be of interest to that user). If users have viewed every one of these articles, the relevance factor is 1. If lower values are reported, this shows lower than expected relevance.

In measuring the relevance factor, it is also important to consider the amount of time spent consuming the content piece and checking that this period reflects what is expected for this content. If someone requests a content page and then immediately clicks on another link and exits the page, it could well mean that the first click was a mistake and that the page is not relevant to the user. If, in contrast, a content page is requested and several seconds pass before the next click, the chances are that something on that page was of interest to the user. Of course, if nothing happens for several minutes, the user has gone away.

Relevance of content for a particular user might have a definite timespan. What is relevant for a user at a particular time might no longer be relevant if the user has fulfilled his of her needs.

If your website contains a search capability, you can analyse the keywords that users type in to reach certain content pieces, and then perform the same searches yourself. This reveals how well your existing content is meeting these requirements, and assists you in spotting the missing content pieces. *Onsite search-effectiveness analysis* is discussed in this chapter on page 126.

Freshness factor

Content freshness measures how 'up-to-date' a site's content is. Content *freshness factor* can be calculated by dividing the average refresh rate of a content area within a given period by the average visit frequency to that content area within the same period. For example, if a content area is refreshed once a week and the average user visits this content area once a week, the user will see fresh content every time he or she visits. A freshness factor of less than 1 means that customers are seeing stale content, as they are visiting more often than you change your content. A freshness factor greater than 1.5 means that your content changes more often than visitors come to the site to view it.

This doesn't mean that every content area needs refreshing. Some content types do not need changing as much—examples include user agreements, privacy statements, and the history of the organisation. In creating each content piece, you should record its expected shelf-life. The interest it generates at the site should be measured against this expected shelf-life. Records of shelf-life will help

---

CASE STUDY
Agora's Online Marketplace
Maintaining the relevance by onsite search-effectiveness analysis

Agora's Online Marketplace can put a process in place to capture and review the search keywords used by participants. The process involves grouping the keywords into categories, repeating searches by the frequently used keywords, and publishing the keywords on the website for the perusal of participants.

Categorising keywords in this way breaks the analysis down into more manageable pieces that are appropriate to particular users of the online marketplace. Repeating the searches helps understanding of how well the website responds to these various keywords. Publishing them on the website informs sellers about what buyers are searching for—such that sellers improve their postings and emphasise their relevant products in line with the searches of buyers.

By implementing this process, Agora learns the terminologies used by the users, and passes on this learning to its participants. All of this makes its service more relevant to sellers and buyers alike.

---

you establish content review times and ensure that your site does not contain old, leftover content pieces.

The fate of old content pieces depends on their type, their relative value to new acquisitions, and their future reference value. You can choose to archive them or you can completely delete them. When new facts override old ones, it is a simple matter of replacement. Seasonal or event-driven content pieces can be completely deleted or can be converted to past tense. For instance, sponsors of the Sydney Olympics covered their involvement extensively before, and during, the Olympics. However, many sponsors still have these pages on their websites a year after the event—without any alterations.

Because the cost of creating the content can be substantial, it is desirable to use methods to extend its shelf-life.

CASE STUDY
Agora's Online Marketplace
Customised content for marketplace participants

When the marketplace participants sign up to Agora's Online Marketplace, they can establish a participant profile which also includes a selection of features that they would like to see when they log-in.

A participant can specify the product lines that are of interest, and these can be displayed as soon as this participant logs-in to the system. This enables the participant to navigate through the list easily, and quickly make decisions on whether he or she wishes to bid or not. In addition, the same participant can opt to see current news items on the same product line—such as buyer and seller announcements in a particular sector, notification of trade fairs, and so on.

In effect, the participant has *customised* the marketplace for his or her use.

Personalisation index
The *personalisation index* is the ratio of the number of profile elements utilised in customer interraction against the number of profile elements collected. A personalisation index greater than 0.75 shows that you make the most of the information you collect, whereas an index less than 0.30 shows that you collect more information than you need—thus wasting resources and possibly annoying visitors.

Personalisation is a broad subject, and is often confused with *customisation*. Both approaches aim to supply appropriate content to the visitor by specifically tailoring the site to appeal to that individual. But there is a distinct difference. A *customisable* site allows the user to set his or her own preferences as to what the site should display. A *personalised* site, in contrast, tries to guess what these preferences are. Both techniques have merits and problems. Each technique achieves different things for different organisations—and in some instances they can be used together in the same website.

Theoretically, a customisable website should be better than a non-customisable one because it eliminates any guessing about what the visitor wants, and gives the user direct ownership of the website experience. But customising a website requires the personal investment of your customer's time. Unless visitors frequently return to the site, this investment is not really justifiable. Ask yourself how many websites you have bothered to customise when the option is available—the answer is probably not many at all. Because an individual visits so many websites, it is not practical to customise all of them. Instead, people tend to concentrate on the few sites that they visit frequently.

This is not to suggest that customisation is a flawed approach to enhancing the appeal of websites. On the contrary, it might be very suitable for some websites, and might be preferred by people with certain online behaviour patterns. It is important to play 'devil's advocate' so you can see the relative merits—and flaws—of customisation before you decide to invest in the technology.

Having said this, there are many problems with the personalisation approach too. The biggest problem is that it relies on an assumption of who the user is. For example, a person might buy a book from amazon.com for a friend. But Amazon has no way of knowing that the book has been bought as a gift and that the buyer, in fact, has no interest at all in the topic or in the style of book purchased. In this case, if Amazon keeps recommending similar titles, the buyer will pay less attention to its recommendations in future.

The way in which personalisation is implemented should not restrict the freedom to choose. Users should drive personalisation. It should not be driven by the software behind the scenes. Perhaps it needs to be a form of 'permission-based personalisation'—if such a thing could exist. If you are implementing personali-sation don't fall into a trap of presumption—such as presuming that a person who buys Levis from your retail oulet on one occasion will never want to buy any other sort of product.

You should always remember that customers buy it—you don't sell it. There might be times when you think you are sure what the customer needs. However, pressing that judgment upon customers is a flawed strategy. You should prepare your content so that your customers state exactly what *they* need or want, as opposed to *your telling* them what they need or want.

The only way to make personalisation work effectively is to understand the purpose of the visit by interacting with the user as pages are being viewed. The use of *cookies* or other script-based mechanisms allows you to identify the user and the session uniquely (see Chapter 9, page 163). When implemented in this way, these techniques are powerful tools, because the entire page can be personalised 'on-the-fly' to present the user with the most suitable content.

Content exposure

Giving away too much information can, potentially, give the game away to your competition. Although there is no easy way to measure content exposure, it is a relevant consideration when producing content.

Many sites, for instance, publish the names and biographies of their key staff members, thus creating good prospecting opportunities for recruitment companies. Alternatively, this might expose their employees to unsolicited salespeople, who tie up staff time in unproductive activity.

Impact on competition

Each major piece of content that you offer creates an impact in the market, especially when it is launched. Checking how it affects the traffic that goes to competitor sites is a useful way to measure how much interest has been created. Reports provided by Internet *traffic-measurement and ranking* services (see Chapter 4, page 85) could be used for this purpose.

DESIGN EFFECTIVENESS

What is missing from web interactions? Listening! Can you make websites listen? This is the designers' challenge!

To make a meaningful contribution to dialogue, we listen first and respond second. The quality of the response reflects our listening ability, and this, in turn, determines the quality of the dialogue. Websites, in contrast, are like a fashion parade—all the outfits are paraded to the viewers without consultation as to whether or not these are the costumes that they want to see.

In the business world, most conversations between organisations, or between a customer and an organisation, require a specific dialogue. First, the customer provides a brief, and then the seller responds with what can be done to service that brief. Another name for this dialogue could be 'interaction'. And, quite often, one interaction is not enough. The customer continues to ask questions, and the seller continues to answer them, until the customer is convinced that there is a strong synergy between his or her need and the seller's value proposition. If the desired synergy is not found, the customer terminates the interaction.

Promoting the value proposition *after* listening to consumer needs is the ideal path to conversion. However, on the Internet, it is a challenging task to listen to what you have heard, to interpret this, and then to customise the value proposition. But it must be done if you want to increase conversion rates.

Face-to-face interactions, whether in a retail outlet or in a meeting with a vendor, are subject to human emotions—involving various aspects of social behaviour and appealing to all senses. Because sight and hearing are the only sensory forms available in web interactions, the focus should be on using these effectively. This means providing analytical tools and features that enable you to 'listen' to your customers. Attempting to incorporate other sensory interactions on your website wastes your creativity and probably deters potential customers.

Consistency between channels is important to establish and maintain trust and brand recognition. However, consistency does not mean that each channel should attempt to replicate the others. Different channels have different attributes with which to work. It is natural that they can offer different features to enhance interactions with customers. Making productive use of different qualities does not undermine consistency.

Comprehensive research shows that behaviours of online users differ substantially. McKinsey and Media Metrics conducted research based on 50 000 users, which suggested that online consumers fall into six segments: 'simplifiers', 'surfers', 'bargainers', 'connectors', 'routiners', and 'sportsters'. Each of these segments exhibits different responses to different design tools. For example, 'simplifiers' dislike pop-up windows that are designed to encourage impulse buying; rather, these 'simplifiers' seek easier and faster ways of doing business. In contrast, according to this research, 'surfers' prefer cutting-edge design.[3]

You might not agree with the detailed conclusions of this research (and its 'categories' of users). However, the research does reinforce the general point that each person behaves differently online. Designers must be aware of this and accommodate these differences in the design and functionality of their sites.

If your website does not 'listen to' (or interact) with the user—based on active listening—any measurement and analysis that you conduct on your website will be after the event. It will not help you to rescue things when they are going wrong, and will enable you only to take action when a similar situation arises next time.

Having understood why people have come to the site (insofar as this can be ascertained), the object of design is to meet their requirements in a simple, succinct, engaging manner. People are extremely goal-driven on the web, and do not tolerate anything standing between them and their goals. The guiding principle for web design must therefore be to keep the site 'clean', so users can achieve their objectives as quickly as possible. This implies *simplicity* and *ease of use*. And the metrics to measure design-effectiveness should be geared towards assessing these two key factors of simplicity and ease of use.

Before considering the metrics, it is important to be aware that the design of a website can *impede* or *enhance* its measurability. Understanding the purpose of a website from a measurability perspective enables designers to create a site that streamlines the measurement process.

As an example of poor design *impeding* measurement, consider how multiple-content pieces on a page can make it impossible to know which content piece the user has sought. Perhaps a lifestyle portal contains a page on Sydney. This page might list various pieces of information that do not lead to any further action—such as the weather forecast, addresses of golf courses, and cinema movie screenings. How would you know which piece of information the user has looked at? Designers should be careful about how they mix different content pieces on a single page.

In contrast, good design can enhance measurability. Implicit user segmentation is an example. On the entry pages of the WebMD site, users are asked to identify themselves as patients or medical practitioners. With the help of design, WebMD therefore knows, in real time, the relative popularity of the site in two distinctly different user types.

Metrics to measure the design effectiveness include:

■ accessibility;
■ scan time;
■ page influence factor;
■ sweet spots; and
■ seducible points.

Each of these is considered below.

Accessibility

Accessibility measures how quickly and easily users can find what they are looking for on a website. It is the measure of how long it takes the average user to navigate to a page and complete a task or conversion. Accessibility depends on *browse path* and *scan time*.

Browse path is the path that the user must take to go from the starting-page to the destination page. The more pages there are between the user and the desired page (the length of the browse path), the more difficult it is to maintain accessibility. A shorter browse path equates to a better chance of conversion.

Scan time, in the sense that it affects accessibility directly, is the time it takes for users to scan each page for the link to the next page, and click on it. When visiting a site, a user takes time on each page to find the link to the next page on the path. The faster the user can find that link on the page, the shorter the overall access time will be. To reduce the scan time, the important links should be positioned higher on the page, so users can find them more easily. Page content should be limited to text and graphics that are absolutely necessary, so links are not hidden in clutter.

Page load-times also affect accessibility, and this is discussed below (see 'Time to build pages', this chapter, page 119).

Usability-testing (see this chapter, page 130) provides additional insight into this metric, and is a method of measuring site accessibility.

Scan time

Scan time, in its broad sense, is the total time that an average user takes to scan and comprehend each design element—such as text, graphics, or multi-media. Scan times should be considered when distributing design elements on a page or across the website, or even on a path to performing a task. It affects site accessibility.

This metric can also be useful in comparing the design composition of a website against other sites. Counting the clicks before a page is fully built helps in assessing the balance of a page's design composition. Pages with higher scores should be revised.

Page influence factor

Page influence is the amount of influence that a page has over the accessibility of other pages. It can be measured by counting how many other pages it links to. The homepage and other entry pages usually have the most influence. Focusing on improving the pages with high influence factor enhances the customer experience.

Sweet spots

Sweet spots are highly visited and sticky pages. Sweet spots can be identified by measuring the duration and frequency of visits to these pages. These pages are the ideal place for critical messages and promotional material, and you can learn a lot from them to improve other pages. Sweet spots are also good starting-points for new users, and organisations should take extra care in planting keywords on these pages so search engines send people straight to them.

Seducible points

Seducible points are the high-risk interaction points where you ask the customer to do something—such as giving his or her credit card number, registering to become a site member, or joining a discussion group. Identifying these pages, and continuously measuring against their stickiness, is an important design consideration.

WEBSITE-PERFORMANCE EFFICIENCY

The technical performance of a website is the baseline requirement for any online initiative. The metrics to measure technical performance should reveal that the website is highly available and functionally efficient.

Typical metrics should include the *availability* of the website, *response-times* to user requests, and the *incidence of errors* (such as broken links). The first is obvious—organisations are seeking to achieve close to 100 per cent site availability. In the context of this discussion, the last two are worth examining further. (Note that optimising a website's technical performance is outside the scope of this book.)

Therefore, the key metrics discussed here to measure performance efficiency are:

∎ the time to build pages; and
∎ the number of errors.

Time to build pages

People who have a slow modem connection often suffer comparatively long load-times. This must be kept in mind when trying to create a visually attractive website. The frustration of waiting for large pages to load can cause dropouts, costing organisations potential customers.

For most webpages, graphics have the largest impact on load-times. Many graphics on the Internet are not optimised for file size. Other objects, such as Java Applets and Flash animations, are also often not optimised. These can be altered to reduce their file size.

It is not only the size of files that affects load-time, but also the number of content pieces on a page. Each file downloaded via the Internet requires a new connection to the webserver, and each of these connections takes time (albeit a short time). The more connections that are required, the slower the overall load-time. Objects that are reused on multiple pages reduce the overall load-time, because they do not have to be downloaded every single time the browser encounters them.

CASE STUDY
Pandora's Online Grocery
Reducing page build-time by effective page composition

Pandora's Online Grocery site is effectively designed—detailed product pages display quickly (taking significantly less than the 8-second benchmark used by many sites) and don't show customers the full product picture unless they click to request it. This is one aspect of design that has allowed Pandora to achieve efficiencies in its website performance.

For the customers, this is important because it means they don't have to wait long to see full product features. Over the course of an entire order this saves a lot of time. For an activity as mundane as grocery shopping, convenience and efficiency are essential to retaining customers.

The speed of a user's connection is an important factor influencing page load-times. However, website operators do not have any control over this. As a benchmark, it is recommended that any webpage should download into a user's browser within a maximum of eight seconds, even on a 56K modem connection. According to Jupiter Communication, 80 per cent of users will still be reaching the Internet through dial-up modems in 2002.[4]

Server-log analytical tools provide insight into periodic load-patterns—such as the number of visitors per hour, per weekday, per season, and so on. This will help you to ensure that there is enough server and line capacity to accommodate visitor peaks. These tools can simulate page loads, and can measure build-times per page and per transaction (including server response-time), broken down by connection speed and compared with the number of dropouts per page.

Visit <www.hurolinan.com> to read the reviews of online *website-performance measurement services* [Locator Code 103]. These services periodically make requests of your webserver and measure server response-times. The operators of the site are alerted, usually via email, when the website returns an error. The errors relate to connection and access to the webserver. In addition, periodic performance reports, which cover various performance metrics (such as server response-times), are also provided.

In addition to the page *load-times*, the *build-order* of pages has a direct impact on dropouts. This is the way that the pages are loaded into the browser. The 'rule of thumb' is to load text first and graphics last. Other considerations for effective build-up and loading of pages should include:

- using framesets for standard navigation to avoid reloading;
- progressively loading images—this can be specified at the time of image creation; and
- using alternative text for images—a simple but very powerful technique in which text appears where the image is going to build, providing a useful description of what the image is, and thus allowing the user to read the descriptive text while the image is loading (and even click on the image before it is fully downloaded).

Number of errors

Once they are launched, websites become living mechanisms. They are in a constant state of change—with the addition of new functionality, modifications to existing functionality, and the removal of unwanted functionality. Any of these changes has the potential to introduce errors in a previously fully tested and functional website. And these errors can cause dropouts.

Comprehensive testing should be embedded into your web-development process. In addition to unit testing of each component of the website, such testing should include integration of the following:

- end-to-end testing of user scenarios or use cases;
- operability testing for page loads at different connection speeds;
- page displays in different browsers and resolutions; and
- eliminating dead-links (also referred to as 'regression testing').

Such an approach should ensure the deployment-worthiness of new components. However, requests for dead-end pages can still occur because of old links provided to a site from external sources. These are outside your testing control. When this happens, browsers display a generic page to the user ('404 error page'—representing the activity status code returned by the webserver), informing the user that the requested page cannot be found. You should consider creating a custom '404 error page' for this purpose. This will increase the chance of keeping the user at your site in spite of a dead page.

Despite precautions and thorough testing procedures, errors still happen. You should closely monitor and fix them as they occur, and this is why they should be assigned a separate metric.

PATH ANALYSIS

Path analysis is the analysis of what users do inside a website, outlining a step-by-step path of the pages visited by a user from the point of entry to when he or she exits the site.

When to use

Path analysis reveals the effectiveness of the information architecture and provides behavioural data about the users of a website. It can be useful for the following purposes:

- finding out how well the navigational elements of a website are working towards reaching the desired outcomes of the site;
- identifying which pages distract the visitors from the desired actions, which pages are potentially confusing, and which pages cause visitors to go in circles or backtrack without reaching the desired actions;
- determining the number of clicks a user takes before performing the desired action; and
- determining possible interests, needs, and behaviours of users by linking the features and functionality that have been consumed.

As a result, you can:

- better organise the critical paths on a website;

Table 6.1 Top-ranking paths on a website

Path number	Path map	Number of sessions	Percentage of total
1	P1 → P2 → P3	3000	24
2	P1 → P3	2000	16
3	P2 → P3	1000	8
4	P1 → P4 → P5 → P6	1000	8
5	P1	875	7
6	P2	250	2
7	P1 → P2	125	1

■ remove intermediate pages to allow impatient visitors to find what they are looking for more quickly;

■ place pages containing important information that would add value to desired actions on higher-ranking paths, thus giving greater exposure to your messages and/or making it easier for visitors to reach desired outcomes; and

■ determine if most visitors follow consistent paths, by comparing the number of sessions for the most popular paths.

How to use

Focusing the analysis on the top paths, or most frequented paths, is a good approach. The example provided in Table 6.1 (above) ranks the top paths in order of usage.

The example in Table 6.1 shows that users might enter the site from either P1 or P2. Entries from pages other than the homepage (paths 3 and 6) might indicate that the user has bookmarked that page (added it to 'favourites'), or that the user has been referred directly from another site. Single page-views, as exhibited in paths 5 and 6, might indicate that the visitors did not find what they were looking for, and have left the site. Alternatively, paths 5 and 6 might suggest that the users found what they were looking for on their entry page, and didn't need any further interaction with the site.

For the non-homepage single page-view, the users might have bookmarked the page (added it to their 'favourites') to get specific information. For the homepage single page-view the users might have visited only for the news headlines. Understanding the significance of these numbers requires comprehensive understanding of both the functionality offered by each page of the website and the needs of your target audience.

Exit pages might indicate whether the visits had a happy ending. In the example shown in Table 6.1, exiting from P3 is common for the top three paths. If P3 is where visitors are expected to leave the site, it is clear that the desired outcome has been achieved in most cases. Moreover, path 2 shows that the website allows for more experienced or impatient users to reach this outcome directly.

A more detailed examination of pages can be conducted by taking a page at a time and looking at the pages visited before and after this page. This will show how visitors find certain pages and what they do after visiting these pages. This analysis is particularly suited to the identification of pages that obstruct the critical path to desired outcomes, or pages that confuse the visitors.

Table 6.2 opposite, shows a detailed examination of P4, which is on path 4 in the example above. Although path 4 ranks relatively highly overall, its pages are not in any other top-ranking paths. So it might be worth examining this page further.

Table 6.2 shows that P4 has been viewed 1000 times in the given period. Of these, 40 per cent of the visits led to users viewing P5, 40 per cent of the visits resulted in users not finding what they were looking for (and consequently leaving the site), and another 20 per cent of the visits resulted in users thinking that they were in the wrong place and going back to P1.

It is also clear from the previous pages visited that the site suffers circular navigation. A significant proportion of visits ended up with the users coming back to P4 (see paths 2 and 3), even after visiting P5 and P6. This might be because the page was used for navigation purposes. It is apparent that if users are not certain about what they are looking for, there is inadequate navigational design on the pages involved. Alternatively, P4 might contain an important piece of content that the users need to refer back to.

Table 6.2 Analysis of paths to and from a webpage

Ref	Percentage of total	Number of sessions	Previous page	Starting-page	Next page	Number of sessions	Percentage of total
1	50	500	P1	P4	P5	400	40
2	35	350	P5		exit	400	40
3	10	100	P6		P1	200	20
4	5	50	entry				

The example provided in Table 6.2 is a generic one. You should do a similar analysis of your website. This is a powerful analytical technique that potentially reveals insightful information about the role played by a website's information architecture in achieving desired outcomes.

There are other ways to utilise the information gleaned from this technique, and these are considered below.

▪ In addition to session numbers, you might consider examining time spent on the paths. But be mindful that duration can mean different things for different paths. For example, a short duration might indicate ease of use in reaching desired outcomes, or it might show that the visitors use the pages only for navigation purposes.

▪ Drilling down from the path to user profiles using *multi-dimensional analysis* (see Chapter 5, page 101) can reveal important information about the composition of visitors who take those paths.

▪ Comparing the results against other time periods can help you understand changes in the interests and preferences of your users. This could be useful for websites that include a wide spectrum of content areas, or where currency of the content is an issue.

▪ Data-cleansing before this analysis is essential. Robots, in particular, will skew the results if their data are not excluded from the analysis—because these programs often scan only what they think are the key pages on a website. Depending on how the pages are linked, this might result in higher values for single page-views. (For more on robots, see chapter 10, page 191.)

■ For content pages that are served dynamically from a database or an external source, an additional level of detail is needed to understand fully what a visitor has looked at. In these circumstances, where the same webpage is used to display different content from a database, linking the content identifiers could be essential for a meaningful interpretation.

■ This technique could be insufficient for websites that employ advanced levels of personalisation, because the path taken by the users will be influenced heavily by the personalisation engine.

■ Many people open multiple browsers as they scan through the one website. This could mean that the same user is taking multiple paths. How this is handled with the software program being used could help you identify when these situations occur.

The prerequisite to *path analysis* is the ability to map all the pages that one user views during a visit. Various techniques can be used to build the linkages—including referrer tags or IP addresses in webserver log files, and session identifiers exclusively created for tracking users.

To perform path analysis, you will probably use a commercial software program. Many of the website-traffic analytical tools offer path analysis as a standard functionality. (These tools are discussed in detail in Chapter 9, pages 176 and 180) Before deciding on a technique, you should evaluate how your pages are linked, because the various techniques offer different degrees of accuracy.

Note that different terms are used to describe path analysis. These include 'clickstream analysis' and 'navigation analysis'. The use of the term 'clickstream' is avoided in the present book because this term is often used in a broader context, referring to overall website-traffic analysis.

ONSITE SEARCH-EFFECTIVENESS ANALYSIS

Onsite search functionality is an integral part of the navigation of a website—and is becoming the centrepiece for some websites. A well-functioning search engine makes the content more accessible to users.

According to a research report from Forrester, 90 per cent of firms rate search as 'very important' or 'extremely important', but 52 per cent do not actually measure its effectiveness.[5] This means that operators of websites do not know if people are finding what they are looking for when they use the search functionality as a way of finding relevant content.

As online content continues to grow, and as users become more experienced in their interactions with websites, search functionality is becoming increasingly popular as a form of navigation within a site. A retailer who participated in the same Forrester research reported that one-third of its traffic is found on the search results page. This is probably in accordance with your own experience as a user in visiting websites. On many occasions, you probably first locate the position of the keyword search functionality.

When to use
As search functionality becomes increasingly commonplace on websites, measurement of its effectiveness becomes more important. Some of the insights possible from this analysis are as follows:

■ discovering the needs of users by assessing what they are searching for;
■ learning users' choice of vocabulary when searching for content on your site;
■ measuring how the search results lead to desired actions; and
■ replicating users' search activity using the same keywords to identify the difference between what they see and what you want them to see.

How to use
Measuring the effectiveness of onsite search functionality involves three activities:

■ defining what you want people to see and what desired actions you want search results to lead to;
■ continuously monitoring how well the search functionality meets the outcomes of the first activity; and
■ aligning the search functionality according to measurement results.

Each of these is considered below.

Defining what you want people to see

The first activity, *defining what you want people to see*, involves a strategic decision and will be different from one site to another. Suffice it to say that you can *limit*, *select*, *categorise*, *prioritise*, and *personalise* the search results.

For example, a retail site can stop the display of a press release about their new range of dairy products when a shopper enters the keyword 'dairy'—thus *limiting* the search results. The same retailer might offer the shopper both higher-priced and lower-priced options in a featured search results section, while listing everything else underneath—thus *selecting* the search results. Again, the same retailer might list the subcategories of dairy products in the search results, as opposed to listing the individual products so that the shopper can drill down themselves—thus *categorising* the search results. Alternatively, the search results might list products in order of price—thus *prioritising* the search results. Finally, placing the brands that the shopper has purchased before at the top of the list is another option—thus *personalising* the search results.

Monitoring the search functionality and outcomes

The second activity requires capturing the keywords used in the searches and *monitoring the outcomes of the searches*. This activity is similar to path analysis (see this chapter, page 122) in many ways, but is triggered by a keyword entered by the user.

Recording the keywords and establishing a mechanism to assess the performance of the site against these keywords is essential for measuring the effectiveness of onsite search functionality. In the Forrester research mentioned above,[6] one of the participant companies performed the search for the top keyword manually, and discovered that the right answer for the top query came in at number 47 on the search results.

For the top keywords in particular, performing manual searches yourself is a valuable process.

Aligning the search functionality

You will occasionally hear site operators complaining that customers are using the 'wrong' keywords in their searches. This is an unwarranted complaint, because organisations should speak the same language as their customers in the first place, and they should be taking the opportunity to learn their customers' terminology from the search keywords.

There are two other things to consider when analysing keywords. First, some of them are seasonal and can expire at any given time—for instance if a popular event has drawn to a close. Second, you should produce metatags from the top keywords for search engine registrations. It is very likely that other people will use the same keywords to search for your site. (For more detailed discussions on search engine registration and defining effective metatags, readers are recommended to refer to the books on this subject.)

Concluding thoughts on search-effectiveness

If the path analysis shows that a lot of people leave the site after they view the search results, you must investigate why. On the one hand, it might mean that your search results show sufficient information to meet your visitor's needs. Conversely, it might indicate that the results are not good enough to entice the user to drill deeper in the site. In the second situation, it could be either that the information returned does not accurately convey the meaning and value of the content kept on the site, or that the content itself is unsatisfactory to the visitors and does not encourage them to look any further.

If the search cannot return any results, you might consider recommending alternatives—which might help you to retain the user. These could include: (i) an advanced search functionality to try again; (ii) displaying an alternative navigation mechanism (such as the site map); or (iii) asking the user's permission to email him or her later when the site *has* developed content on the search keyword.

Search functionality is significant for many websites. If you are the operator of one of these sites, your can choose to build it in-house, or you can use a commercially developed program. Regardless of your choice, you should ensure that the activities performed on the search functionality are measured for effectiveness.

USABILITY-TESTING

Usability-testing is the measurement of how well a website aligns with the behaviours of online users, enabling them to complete their tasks efficiently, effectively, and satisfactorily.

When to use

By paying attention to usability, you will be able to refine your site so that when people come to your website, they will be able to find what they are looking for—and find it easily. Usability-testing can be used as a tool for diagnosis and comparison in the following ways:

▪ understanding if the customers can complete tasks satisfactorily and in a timely manner;

▪ detecting obstacles that prevent customers from reaching desired outcomes; and

▪ comparing the time and effort required to complete tasks on your website with that required on competitor sites and industry best-practice sites.

How to use

Organisations should perform usability-testing throughout all phases of a website's life—(i) during the development process; (ii) when preparing to introduce major functionality changes, and (iii) when it is fully operational.

Usability-testing is a building-block in developing websites. Organisations should first establish that the web designers working on the project understand the accepted usability principles and can incorporate them into your site's design. If the organisation has had a prior web presence, usability-testing offers insights into their successes and failures.

You can pick up what works well and what doesn't, and modify the new design accordingly. Such a study, although it might seem like an extra investment in the first instance, is actually money well spent. It can deliver savings later on by helping to retain your existing customers during the conversion to a new site design. Later, the site prototype should be usability-tested to show whether you have the design right, and whether your customers can reach their end goals easily.

Usability-testing is a method of measuring website accessibility—a metric that was discussed in design effectiveness (see this chapter, page 114). It usually involves analysing how people from a test panel of your target audience reach specific goals in a laboratory environment. Usability consultants observe how the test panel members move their mouse and their eyes over the screen. This indicates which areas of the webpage attract attention, and which tend to be overlooked. The test panel can perform the same activities on competitors' sites and industry best-practice sites to provide comparison.

Conducting usability-testing is a proactive step. It will help you anticipate how suitable the website is for the target audience. If the website performs well in the testing phase, you have a level of assurance that the website will work. However, if it returns possible hiccups, you can modify the site to improve the experiences of customers. Organisations should seek practical results from usability-testing—results that can produce constructive remedial action.

Usability-testing requires specialist skills. Depending on the size and maturity of your online initiatives you might procure these services from external service providers. The operators of larger websites might choose to employ full-time, in-house usability consultants.

Although there is much to be gained from usability-testing, it is not enough on its own.

First, the website design should guide, encourage, persuade, influence, and assist potential customers to go in a specific direction. And this direction is dictated by the purpose of your website. If you are serious about your online initiatives, they should represent much more than simply being a customer self-service point—they are part of your customer-engagement toolkit and have significant effects on your customer relationships.

Second, usability-testing alone cannot measure the success of a website. It is one of the good tools, but it is unsafe to extrapolate the results of such studies to the total audience. Once operational, you should closely monitor how well the customer experience aligns with the capabilities of the site. You can do this

Visit <www.hurolinan.com> to find the details of *usability-testing consultants* and *online usability service providers* [Locator Code 104]. Online service providers use intelligent agents to perform task analysis. These simulate the behaviours of a web user to analyse a specific task within a website.

through usability-testing in conjunction with the other metrics and analytical techniques provided in this book.

SUMMARY

There are three underlying factors that influence dropouts from the customer-engagement stages—*content appropriateness*, *design effectiveness*, and *website-performance efficiency*. Each of these factors has a set of metrics and analytical tools that can help you determine the role they play in retaining—or losing—customers. Understanding these factors, and measuring and analysing their effects on your website, is a proactive strategy to eliminate the factors that might cause dropouts in future.

Three analytical techniques were provided in this chapter:

▌ *path analysis*—to organise better the critical paths on a website (by identifying and removing obstacles that can cause dropouts);
▌ *onsite search-functionality effectiveness*—to discover what the users are looking for, and to ensure that the search results lead to desired outcomes; and
▌ *usability-testing*—to understand if the customers can complete their tasks on a website satisfactorily and in a timely manner.

CHAPTER

7

Choosing Metrics and Analytical Techniques

The value of measurement relies on how much the business performance will benefit from the results. If the organisation cannot strategically act on the results, the process will be merely an assurance tool that does not lead to any substantial returns. In deciding the size and scope of proposed measurement activities, an organisation should balance the expected value of those activities against their costs, and should assess what might happen in the absence of measurement.

Establishing a web-measurement practice for your site can be a significant project involving various costs. These costs include the following.

■ *Tools for data collection and analysis:* The sophisticated systems used for data collection, integration, and analysis all cost money. As yet, package systems that cover all aspects of management are not readily available, and therefore organisations need to select multiple tools (perhaps develop be-spoke systems), and integrate them to implement a sophisticated measurement system. Chapter 12 (page 211) discusses the tools required for measurement.

■ *Procurement of external data and analysis results from third-party companies:* Organisations might decide to outsource data collection, using vendor services to complement or replace in-house measurement practices. The cost of these services should be factored into the considerations. Chapter 12 (page 211) discusses the outsourcing options available to organisations.

■ *Complexities involved in data collection:* Measurement that requires integration of data from multiple sources is more costly, because it requires the establishment of data elements to form the relationships among the data sources—with the removal of inconsistent and overlapping data, and the creation of a platform to integrate the data. Chapter 10 (page 193) provides a checklist for data integration from multiple sources.

■ *Resource and time commitments:* Web measurement requires specialist skills that are not widely available in the market. The cost of procuring these skills should be factored into the cost considerations. Chapter 11 (page 202) discusses the skill requirements and roles of web analysts.

The present chapter discusses the factors that influence the choice of metrics and analysis for different websites.

Metrics and analytical techniques are two of the core components of website measurement. You can consider *web metrics* to be like a health check-up, whereas *analytical techniques* are like diagnostic surgery, opening up the website to discover the causes of the metrics' results.

The process establishes action points which, when implemented, will improve the website and its associated offline initiatives. For example, a metric might show the cost of acquiring a customer. By multi-dimensional analysis (see Chapter 5, page 101), one can then drill down into the components of this cost and identify techniques that attract more targeted customers from a particular segment. The organisation can concentrate its resources on these identified techniques.

CHOOSING THE RIGHT METRICS

Every website is unique. Just as no two online strategies are exactly alike, so no two metrics programs should be the same—even within the same industry. Because different organisations have different business strategies and priorities, they engage in different online activities. What is important for one organisation to measure might not be at all important for another.

Drivers for selecting metrics

Business managers responsible for online initiatives should take an active role in selecting metrics and in formulating actions arising from the measurement results. To identify the most important metrics, organisations should consider the following:

▮ business strategies;
▮ maturity of the online initiative; and
▮ degree of integration.

Each of these is considered below.

Business strategies

The first driver for selecting metrics relates to *business strategy*. The focus of the metrics essentially depends on the primary online processes of an enterprise. For example, a customer-intimate enterprise should evaluate its capability to support sales and customer-care processes. In contrast, an organisation competing on

Table 7.1 Critical web processes based on value principle

Value discipline	Key business metrics	Most critical web-based process (to be managed for greatest value)
Operational excellence	Cost per transaction Defect rate Cycle time Inventory turn	Supply-chain management Sourcing Procurement Inventory and order management
Product leadership	Product performance Time to market	Collaborative design Knowledge management
Customer intimacy	Share of wallet Cross-sell rate Customer satisfaction	Customer service Sales support
Brand mastery	Brand equity Brand awareness Brand perception	Marketing Online advertising

Source: D. Flint & D. Cirillo, *WebAnalytics: Getting Down to Business*, Gartner Research Note SPA–13–5394, April 2001, Gartner Inc.

operational efficiency should focus on back-end processes, such as order fulfilment and supply-chain efficiency. As a further example, product innovators will want to examine progress in knowledge management.

Table 7.1 (above) shows examples of key metrics for each value and highlights the most critical web-based processes. These processes should receive priority in analysis and be managed for greatest value.

Maturity of online initiatives

The second driver for selecting metrics relates to *maturity of online initiatives*. The starting-point for most enterprises when developing a web presence is brochure-ware. This passive web presence is progressively enhanced to provide interaction, usually with customers and prospects. Clearly, a brochure-ware site, which is no different from other marketing collateral that the organisation creates, requires only limited metric support. The only real measurables are basic traffic data—such as page-views displayed, unique sessions, and duration of visits.

As a website matures and becomes more complex, more sophisticated metrics should be used to measure the level of participation and interaction. Such metrics might include postings on a discussion board, subscriptions to newsletters, and so on.

When enterprises begin to offer transactions online, the value of web activity grows, and additional metrics are justified. These organisations can use metrics to ensure successful completion of transactions.

Degree of integration

The third driver for selecting metrics relates to *degree of integration*. To provide end-to-end solution, and to achieve transaction efficiency, many websites closely integrate with other sources of data, processes, and software applications. Organisations with these integrated websites should select metrics that indicate the success of integration. For example, an organisation might give its customers the option of moving to other channels to complete the transaction. This organisation should devise metrics that demonstrate the effect of cross-channel travels—for example a measure of how much influence the website has on offline channels.

Confirming measurability

Having considered the *drivers* for choosing the right metrics, we now turn to the importance of confirming measurability. Metrics measurement involves the collection of the underlying data, followed by the calculation of the metric result. Business managers and web analysts should agree on the data source and the calculation formula. In discussing this, they will verify that the metric is measurable. If not, it will be necessary either to change the metric definition or to investigate new methods of collecting the necessary data.

This is an important process that should be completed early, because it realises the value of your selected metrics. Data source and standard measurement units are discussed in Chapter 8 (page 150).

Setting target values for metrics

Apart from *drivers* and *confirmation of measurability* (considered above), to gauge the level of website performance, it is necessary to *compare the results of metrics against their expected values*. This reflects the importance of budgeting or forecasting. The expected values should be available in, or derived from, the business case assessment for the online initiative.

Failing to set expected values will limit your ability to benchmark the performance against what the online initiative is set to achieve. It might be necessary to revisit and update the expected results once the online initiative is operational and being measured. These changes should be reflected in the business plan.

Reviewing the choice of metrics

Part of the ongoing process of choosing the right metrics (see above, this chapter) is a proper *review* of these metrics at appropriate intervals. This involves consideration of:

■ lifespan of metrics;
■ relationships among metrics; and
■ effects of external factors on web metrics.

Each of these is considered below.

Lifespan of metrics

In choosing and reviewing metrics, it is important to appreciate that metrics have a shelf-life, and will therefore expire. They should be reviewed periodically, and enhanced or replaced as appropriate to their *lifespan*.

There is a clear correspondence between the growth of your website and the sophistication of the metrics. When you launch a website, you have progressed to a new phase in your eBusiness strategy, a phase which incorporates learning and growth. Growth occurs as you learn more about the site, as its tangible benefits appear, and as it stabilises. The metrics are similar: once you start measuring them you will establish that many of them remain predictable or constant over time. This is the time to look for other things to measure.

The need for enhancement or replacement of a metric can occur for several reasons.

∎ The stability of the metric over a reasonable period of time might free resources to start focusing on new metrics—metrics that provide different insights into your website.
∎ The need for measuring different aspects of a metric or replacing it completely might arise if the metric frequently returns unpredictable and inconsistent results.
∎ The objective of your website will be changed by strategic changes in the product or service offerings of your organisation, or by the way in which your organisation wants to use online channels. This changing objective will require you to review your existing metrics and, potentially, to devise a new set of metrics.
∎ Major changes in the form of content, functionality, and design might require that you measure different aspects of your site.

Relationships among metrics

In choosing and reviewing metrics, apart from the shelf-life of metrics (see above) it is important to appreciate the *interrelationships among metrics*. Just as the measurement framework reflects a complicated relationship—with many inter-dependencies—between a business and its customers, the metrics also have interdependencies with one another. The outcomes of your activities in one stage directly affect the outcomes in other stages. Well-designed metrics will show this. Drilling down from one metric to another within the same stage, and then across stages, could reveal important information. You can learn even more if you link the metrics of one channel with the metrics of another.

Different metrics might have an underlying dependency on each other. Attempting to fix the problems suggested by poor performance in one metric can have a positive or negative impact on other metrics. If you are making changes to your website's functionality, content, and design, you should maintain a holistic approach that monitors the impact of changes on all metrics. Changes should have a positive or neutral impact on metrics—although occasionally a sacrificial negative impact on one metric is unavoidable. To measure the impact after major changes have been made, a form of post-implementation review is critical. For example, removing user log-ins from a content category of a website might increase the session numbers and page-views for the content area, but it might also have implications for your ability to identify the users and perform other analyses.

Effects of external factors on web metrics

Finally, in choosing and reviewing metrics, apart from *lifespan* and *interrelationships* (both considered above), it is important to appreciate the *effects of external factors* on various metrics. No business operates in isolation. The actions of your business create an impact, however small, in the broader market, just as the actions of your competitors create an impact. External factors—such as government policies and regulations, international conflicts, fluctuations in financial markets, and major sporting or political events—also affect the market and can potentially influence the performance of your business. If you are aware of these influences, and incorporate their impact into your measurements, you will generate more realistic results.

Internet traffic measurement—offered by many service providers—can be used to detect and explain the business effects of such trends and external factors. Similarly, you can use the services to understand the impact that your business is creating in the market.

For more detailed discussion on Internet traffic-measurement services, see Chapter 4 (page 85).

CHOOSING THE RIGHT ANALYTICAL TECHNIQUE
Summarising the analytical techniques

A number of analytical techniques can help you to understand how well your website is performing, and thus enable you to plan future activities better. The advantages and disadvantages of each technique, and the issues involved, have been discussed in detail in the previous chapters.

Table 7.2 (page 142) summarises the available analytical techniques, and where further information can be found on each of them in this book.

Deciding to use analytical techniques

Organisations might decide to implement some of these analytical techniques as part of standard measurement practices, or on a case-by-case basis to answer specific questions, explain erratic performance results, or prepare for new online or offline activities.

You need to know what techniques to use well in advance because the techniques might require special technology or set-up (especially in areas such as data collection). A good example is multi-dimensional analysis. You will not be able to do this properly unless you have an online analytical processing (OLAP) tool. In addition, for multi-dimensional analysis, you need to establish relationships among the data elements. If you collect data arbitrarily, and then decide to perform this analysis, establishing these relationships can be a long and expensive task—oftentimes impossible. You therefore need to know in advance that you will be performing this sort of analysis.

Any analysis, if it is to reveal important aspects of your website, requires the procurement of tools and services from external companies, as well as the time and resources of your organisation.

Verifying analysis results
Before drawing any serious conclusions from results, much less acting upon them, it is important to verify analysis results. These results might indicate a need to make changes to the website or its associated activities. Before effecting any of these changes, you should confirm the anticipated value of them.

The nature of the planned change will affect how it can be verified. There could be many ways to verify the results, including:

- another analytical technique such as usability-testing;
- focus group meetings with customer representatives; and
- online surveys.

When the verification method involves user participation, it is critical to find a demographic match between the test group used to confirm the results and the user base from which the original results were inferred. This will deliver meaningful conclusions.

Table 7.2 Summary of analytical techniques

Technique	What it does	Why use it?
Best customer analysis (see page 80)	categorises online customers based on frequency and recency of visits, and monetary value of customers	to target activities or personalise website content more closely to customer segments; and to forecast future usage of website and monetary value of online activities
Customer-engagement funnel (see page 83)	visualises the engagement performance with customers in terms of customer numbers and monetary values	to consolidate certain metrics; to identify bottlenecks; and to forecast high-level customer activities in the future
Internet traffic-measurement and ranking (see page 85)	compares high-level traffic data (such as page-views and sessions) to similar sites; based on reports produced by web-traffic measurement companies	to understand and compare usage values of similar sites; and, possibly, to explain the effect of external features on rapid changes in the website usage
Where from—to analysis (see page 87)	identifies which sites the users visited immediately before and after visiting a website	to gauge effectiveness of online activities that are used to generate traffic to a website
Multi-dimensional analysis (see page 101)	examines the results of a metric in relation to other data elements, to explain the factors that might impact upon the metric result	to obtain greater understanding of metric results so that the activities to improve their performance are better aligned can be used in conjunction with many of the other techniques to provide a drill-down facility

Path analysis (see page 122)	maps a step-by-step path of the pages visited, from the point of entry to a website to its exit page	to find out how well navigational elements of a website contribute towards reaching the desired outcome
Onsite search-effectiveness analysis (see page 126)	analyses the effectiveness of onsite search functionality	to gauge how well the search functionality on a website works; and to learn about users' needs and their choices of termi-nology from the searches conducted
Usability-testing (see page 129)	measures how well a website aligns with the online behaviours of users	to understand if the customers can complete their tasks on a website satisfactorily and in a timely manner

Online surveys

Online surveys are commonly used as a technique for confirming analysis results.

The fundamental problem with online surveys is that they are self-recruiting. This almost guarantees a certain demographic bias and the attraction of people with a particular motivation.

Research shows that young users are overrepresented in online surveys. A recent online survey conducted by the Australian Broadcasting Corporation's (ABC) website revealed that one of the ABC's radio stations, Triple J, attracted most of the participants.[1] The results were therefore skewed towards the preferences of that demographic group—which is composed of young people who are politically aware (and perhaps politically active) and who have non-mainstream musical taste.

Sophisticated solutions are now available. These significantly reduce demographic bias and lead to higher response rates. These randomly invite users to complete surveys, or base surveys on rules that include user profiles and specific actions conducted by users at a website.

The design of online surveys is important in obtaining results. Concise, clear questions, which might involve asking respondents to confirm preferences or opinions, will help procure comprehensive analysis results.

IMPLEMENTING THE ACTIONS

Two important activities should accompany the implementation of changes arising from analysis—*piloting* and *communication*. In principle, measuring the effectiveness of website content does not differ from the testing of marketing messages and campaigns in other customer channels.

Piloting

By developing a *pilot* you can trial the change on a sample of users (random or selected), and identify whether your desired outcomes are achieved. This allows for fine-tuning before a full-scale launch. The magnitude of the change being considered dictates the importance of piloting and the resources committed to it.

Communication

The expected impact of the change on the existing users determines whether the proposed changes should be *communicated* to them. It is a good practice to communicate the changes to users, allowing them to experience them and provide feedback in advance of their full-scale launch. Increasingly, websites are providing links to new design and navigation concepts before launching them. This is good practice because it creates an opportunity for monitoring and responding to feedback while the interested users are familiarising themselves with the new design.

SUMMARY

Metric results and subsequent analysis should lead to practical outcomes. The value of measurement lies in the practical implementation of its outcomes. Unless you can produce outcomes, the measurement produces no return.

Inability to deduce practical outcomes that improve business performance indicates problems with your web-measurement practices.

Metrics reveal the website's performance, and to explain these results you must perform analysis. There are several analytical techniques available that can provide insight to help explain the results. You can then identify, where appropriate, practical outcomes to improve performance.

Metrics for an online initiative should be specifically tailored to particular websites. Choosing a suitable and balanced set of metrics is influenced by factors such as: (i) deciding how much to measure; (ii) the business strategies; (iii) the maturity of the online initiative; and (iv) the level of integration with offline and other online initiatives.

To gauge the level of performance, it is necessary to compare metrics results against their expected values. The process of defining each metric requires specification of the formula to calculate the results, and specification of the data required for this calculation. The formula and the data sources should be verified to ensure measurability. Metrics have a limited lifespan, interdependencies differ, and their performance can be influenced by external factors.

To explain the performance of the metric results, analysis must be performed. There are several analytical techniques available. Through these techniques you can fully understand the causes of a metric's results and identify, where appropriate, practical outcomes to improve its performance.

Some of the techniques are also suitable as planning tools for online and offline initiatives, and can predict the likely outcomes of future activities.

PART

3

Data Collection, Cleansing, and Integration

CHAPTER

8

Understanding the Data

The data chosen to measure metrics and perform analysis should be closely linked to the measurement needs of the website. Organisations should not collect data simply because they can, as the measurement results gathered from such unplanned data collection can be misleading, not to mention a waste of time and resources. Organisations should always seek to understand the purpose of data collection, and how it will help to measure the success of the website.

The evolution of the Internet has spawned a number of new measurement terms, most of which are yet to be standardised. This chapter provides definitions of these measurement units.

Websites have come a long way since brochure-ware first appeared on the Internet. There are now layers of application components in most websites, ranging from content-management systems to commerce servers. Each component offers new types of data about interactions with users. Depending on the technical complexity of the website, it might be necessary to collect and integrate data from multiple layers to calculate the metrics results. This chapter also discusses these layers and the scope for data collection from each layer.

At the core of any user interaction with a website is the webserver. Regardless of the application layer used, the user interacts with the webserver, and the webserver manages the provision of the functionality with other application layers. Finally, therefore, as a foundation for understanding the collection of user-activity data, this chapter discusses how the webpages are served to users.

DEFINING UNITS OF MEASUREMENT

Providing definitive units of measurement is an important part of the web-measurement process. Many, if not all, of the web metrics we use rely on these definitions to obtain accurate measurement. Even though there are no industry standards for such definitions as yet, suggested definitions are outlined in Table 8.1 opposite.

When you start investigating the possibilities of what might happen during a visit or page-view, and try to cater for any exceptions that might occur, these definitions can become complex and confusing. Progress in standardising them is

Table 8.1 Basic measurement terms

Term	Suggested definition
User	A person who accesses a website; a user might be responsible for multiple visits to the site over a period of time, or open multiple sessions during one visit.
Session	A series of page views requested from the website by the same user in an unbroken sequence.
Visit	A specific visit to a website that ends when the user has taken no further action after a given period of time—usually 30 minutes—indicating he or she is no longer at the site; a user might open multiple sessions of the website during a single visit.
Page-view	A request for the display of a full-page document, a webpage (rather than an element of a page such as an image, movie, or audio file) on a website.
Hit	A single entry in a server log file, generated when a user requests a resource on a website; hits are not a useful comparison between websites or parts of the same website and should not be used as a measurement unit, as each webpage is made up of an arbitrary number of individual files.

hampered by debates about how to handle these exceptions. For example, do you consider it a 'page-view' if the page has not been fully served and the user has decided to abandon the page by moving on to something else? Technically, this is not a 'page-view'. However, it might be that you have presented your content in a sequence desired by the user and the user has already clicked on a link to look at something else, or has perhaps already bought the product. In this light, the final result might well be deemed to have been a successful 'page-view'.

Are standard definitions really necessary? It would certainly save time and improve communication if there were widely accepted terms, but standardisation is a tough road with little prospect for success. Although some people always strive to standardise, others always try to *differentiate* their products and services—to protect them from becoming commoditised. This differentiation also prevents these products being measured against their competition. Therefore, although there have been many attempts towards standardisation (of definitions, product codes, and so on), these projects have failed. Without some sort of legislative authority enforcing the standards, the chances of standardisation are very slim.

Without a standard set of terms to draw from, you should aim at establishing definitions *within* your organisation, and communicate these to all persons involved in the measurement process. As you are measuring the effectiveness of your website for the benefit of your organisation, its customers, and other stakeholders, you should ensure that all of these parties are clear on the definitions of the terms you are using.

UNDERSTANDING DATA SOURCES

A key component of defining metrics is the specification of the data required. This activity will reveal what data are available for measurement and what additional data need to be captured. If data are not readily available, a method to capture these data should be specified, whether it be additional programming or alterations to the design or functionality.

Unfortunately, as websites have evolved from brochure-ware and standard HTML, the process of collecting data has become more complex.

Websites now provide dynamic content, which is stored in databases and managed by applications. They are often integrated with other online and offline corporate applications to enable business processes; and are sometimes integrated with external service providers for the processing of payments and transactions, the publishing of content, and advertisement serving.

In such a complex web environment, a company might use multiple layers of technology, each supplying a new data source of user interactions. Table 8.2 (opposite) illustrates some of these data sources.

Table 8.2 demonstrates that it is possible to collect data from all aspects of your site's interactions with online customers—from viewing simple content pages to

Table 8.2 Data sources for measurement

Data source	What does it do?	What data types?
Webserver	receives user requests to view a webpage; delivers the page to the browser based on hypertext transfer protocol (http)	user-activity data with websites
Content server	stores and presents content dynamically to websites; sometimes integrated with personalisation or ad servers to supply more relevant content	content consumption data by users
Catalogue server	stores product information and supplies shopping-cart functionality; often integrated with ad servers, personalisation servers, or commerce servers to construct product listing	shopping-behaviour profiles of customers
Commerce server	supports sales, payments, tax calculations, shipping and handling; often integrated with third services to provide end-to-end transaction fulfilment	operational-performance data
Personalisation server	leverages customer/ prospect profiles to match user with targeted content and commerce promotions	user-needs profile
Ad server	local or externally hosted server that dispenses advertisements	advertising-performance data and information on user interests and needs
Exchange server	business-to-business network for buying and selling goods; supplier information is mostly formatted in XML, for sharing and processing with an exchange or corporate supplier network	operational-performance data

responding to advertisements displayed. This is good news for organisations that have traditionally found it difficult to understand who their customers are. To benefit from this wealth of information, organisations should define what information they capture and store it in relevant sections of their customer-knowledge systems.

Each server can log activities. During implementation, organisations should be mindful of how the activities logged by different servers can be integrated. This involves identifying data elements that would provide the linkage between log data, consolidating these data with the rest of their customer-knowledge systems, and cleansing overlapping data.

Regardless of the complexity of the technology layers, it is the webserver that plays the central role in interactions with end-users. Webservers act as a filter between the user and the functionality offered by other servers. In order words, users first make their requests to webservers, and webservers negotiate these requests elsewhere. The following section provides a detailed discussion on webserver activities and important aspects of data collection from these servers.

SERVING WEBPAGES TO USERS

The basic activity of online interaction involves a user requesting a specific action on a website. As such, this is the primary activity recorded in web measurement. To initiate the request the end-user might use browser software or any other Internet device. Whatever he or she uses, this is referred to as 'client software'. The webserver, on which the website resides, is responsible for responding to this request.

Webpages are served to the end-user in various ways. The most common involves the user's request being communicated via the Internet directly to the webserver, and the page then being served from there. However, this is not always the case.

The proxy servers at the Internet service provider (ISP) or at the user's place of work might have cached the webpage, and might serve it from there. Proxy servers act as a 'go-between', mediating between an organisation and the Internet. They aim to improve performance by filling a request directly—if the necessary information is available—rather than forwarding the user to the Internet. Proxy servers also block unauthorised activity—both outgoing and incoming—and are otherwise known as 'firewalls'. If the user is accessing the Internet from behind a firewall—a practice common to most workplace systems—the firewall is directly negotiating the requests with the webservers, instead of the user's computer doing this. The request is communicated to the firewall software, which then requests the activity from the webserver on the user's behalf.

In some other cases, the user's own browser might have cached the contents of the webpage and might check the update status on the webserver. If no updates have occurred it can serve the requested page directly from its cache, without communicating the request to the ISP and the webserver.

The user can use the backwards and forwards keys in the browser software to look at the pages that were previously viewed. In this case, these pages will be served from the memory of the user's own computer.

These methods of serving webpages to users recur frequently. When they do, the webservers are unaware of the activity that is occurring, and therefore cannot log the details. This situation is more of a problem for webpages that contain static content. After the first visit, it is likely that subsequent visits will be missed by the webserver because the content will be delivered directly from user's cache. If the webpage contains content that is changed frequently, the caching is overridden, and the request is again served from the webserver.

Figure 8.1 (page 156) illustrates the various possibilities that arise when a user requests a webpage.

The above discussion is based on the assumption that the entire contents of a website sits on the one webserver. This might not be the case, especially for larger websites, as they can span multiple webservers. If this is so, when the user navigates through the website, they might jump from one webserver to another without knowing.

It is also possible that the same website (or even a page on a website) might supply content and features from external sources. These are known as

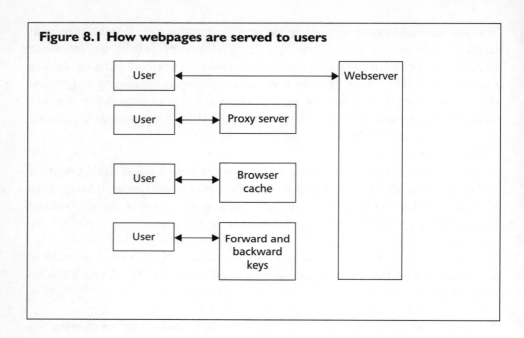

Figure 8.1 How webpages are served to users

'composite websites' and, again, the requests made by the user for a single webpage display will be responded to by multiple webservers.

The architectural aspects of Internet communications also make it possible to collect the same data at different points—for example, at the client or server layer. Having multiple sources for the same or similar data that could be used for the same purpose imposes a challenging situation. For the purposes of web measurement, this demands that organisations clearly define data-collection strategies.

SUMMARY

Data required to measure metrics and perform analysis should be closely linked to the measurement needs of the website. Organisations should not collect data simply because they can, and they should be wary of using measurement results gathered from an unplanned data collection. Such measurement is a waste of time and resources. Before undertaking any measurement, organisations should delineate what the purpose of data collection is, and how it will assist in measuring the success of the website.

The evolution of the Internet has spawned a number of new measurement terms. There are, as yet, no standard definitions for these terms. However, they are required for measuring some of the metrics that your organisation will choose to use. Do not wait for standardisation efforts to be successful. Pick the definitions suitable for your organisation and communicate these to all persons involved in the measurement process.

Websites have come a long way since brochure-ware first appeared on the Internet. There are now complex layers of application components in most websites, ranging from content-management systems to commerce servers. Each component offers new types of data about interactions with users. Depending on the technical complexity of the website, it might be necessary to collect and integrate data from multiple layers to calculate the metrics results.

Central to any web-measurement practice is the study of the activity that takes place between a browser and a webserver. This best illustrates a user's inter-action with a website, and is essential to web measurement.

CHAPTER 9

Collecting
the Data

The underlying data for many metrics stem from the details of inter-actions that take place between the user and the website. This is called *user-activity data*.

The primary mechanism to link the activities of the same user in the user-activity data is through *user identities*. Although this does not necessarily imply knowing the name and address details of the user, it does mean the ability to distinguish the activities of different users. There are several techniques to identify users of a website, and these produce results of varying richness and accuracy. The first part of this chapter discusses these techniques, contrasting their differences and detailing examples of situations in which they are suitable.

User-activity data can be captured at three distinct points—webserver, browser, or network. Each data-collection point has unique implications for measurement results and involves different levels of complexity. The second part of this chapter discusses these data-collection points, detailing the implications of choosing one collection point rather than another as the data source of user activities.

The concept of customer-centricity implies a need to get closer to customers. To achieve this, you must learn more about your customers, which is only possible through data collection. The web is an ideal medium for this. When customers interact with websites, it is possible to track everything they do. However, the ethics of the unauthorised acquisition and use of personal information is a heavily debated topic. The final section in this chapter discusses the privacy implications of data collection.

IDENTIFYING THE USERS

To realise the objectives of your online initiative, you need to answer three key questions about your customers:

■ Who are they?
■ What are their needs?
■ What sort of online behaviours do they exhibit?

You have probably already gathered a lot of information about existing customers from other channels, and this will help to answer the first two questions. This knowledge will also help you engage customers in the online channels, as these existing customers start using your website. The last question (above) is more difficult to answer, because it involves understanding the behaviours of customers in the online channels. Since this is a relatively new medium for any organisation, not much information exists.

Your initial thought might be that a thorough understanding of customers is necessary only for organisations running complex websites, which offer detailed transactions to customers. This thinking is wrong. Even if you operate the simplest of the websites—for example, a brochure-ware site that contains only corporate information such as the company name, a description of business products and services, and locations of offices or outlets—you want to know who is visiting your site. If you have no means of knowing who is looking at your site and how well it is serving their needs, and if you have no inclination to learn, there is no point in having the site in the first place. If you can't measure its value, don't set it up.

Of course, you have to be realistic. There are budgetary constraints attached to everything you do, and the amount of time and money you invest in capturing and analysing this information depends on the value of the information to your business. This, in turn, relates to the ultimate purpose of your website. However, regardless of budget, you should be performing some form of measurement.

Discovering the users' behaviours involves the ability to identify each customer when he or she visits your website, and the ability to cross-reference this identification to your organisation's customer database. Many traditional companies already hold a lot of electronic information about their customers, and this can potentially be linked to online channels when the customers use these new channels. There are many practical ways of identifying existing customers when they come to your websites, but the companies that have identification techniques in place—ones that are clearly visible to the customers—are in the best position.

Airlines, utility companies, and banks fall into this category. And users expect these companies to hold this information because they need to access individual account information. For example, airlines use frequent-flyer numbers to identify customers, and utilities use account numbers to access their customers' records.

CASE STUDY
Updating frequent-flyer records

I was shocked when I first visited my airline's website. When I looked at my personal profile, I realised how little this company knew about me, and how out of date its knowledge of me was. My personal records showed exactly the same information that I had provided to the airline many years ago when I had submitted my application form for frequent-flyer points. Although I didn't stop flying with this airline after making this discovery, I was disappointed that the airline apparently had no process in place to update the information held about me in its database.

As a good customer who believes in 'win-win' arrangements with his vendors, I updated my personal records on the site myself, entering new information that the airline didn't have—such as my new telephone numbers, my email address, and my seat preferences. In doing this, I felt that I was in charge of maintaining my own profile. As I was entering the information directly into my airline's system, I felt more confident that the information it had about me was correct and up-to-date, and more assured that it would be able to serve me better in the future. For instance, the airline now knew to give me an aisle seat, which is very important to me because I often need to stretch my legs.

But think about it also from the perspective of the airline. It has shifted the burden of collecting and maintaining quality data about a customer—which can be an expensive process—to the customer himself. The airline's check-in staff will be spared a lengthy discussion, possibly fraught with emotion, about getting an aisle seat every time I fly. This increases the throughput of customers at the check-in desk, reduces the stress of check-in staff, and increases my customer satisfaction. The airline now knows my phone numbers and correct address if it needs to contact me.

This example, although it might seem trivial, is a good illustration of how a company can start from its existing knowledge of customers and can enhance this using the online channel. The lesson here? The web can be used to collect quality data about an organisation's customers.

However, although they have easy access to identification methods, they don't necessarily use them, as the case study on the updating of frequent-flyer records shows.

Registration forms

Not every company is as fortunate as airlines, banks, and utility companies. Many businesses lack established mechanisms to identify customers uniquely, and even if they have internal practices in place, such as customer numbers, these could never be passed on to the customers. For one thing, if customers were given these numbers, they could not keep track of them for all the companies they interact with. Another problem with using existing internal customer numbers for identification is that they are usually assigned only to customers who have already had transactions with the organisation. Such numbers are not used to identify prospective customers. To use a number to identify prospects it would be necessary to assign numbers to people in the *reach* stage, and to create a new customer record in your back-end system for each person visiting your website.

So there is a need for a common form of user identification that enables websites to identify their users. And this identification method cannot be dictated by the business—it must be decided by the user.

The solution that is proving most popular for websites in identifying users is the use of email addresses. This is both logical and simple—each person knows his or her email address, and no two addresses are the same. However, an issue arises when a person changes that email address, as occurs frequently for many people. The resolution for this issue is simple as well—the website offers a mechanism for updating these details.

From the organisation's point of view, this is as good as it gets. An email address not only helps in uniquely identifying visitors to its website, but also allows the business to communicate with its customers online (subject to the agreement of the visitor). Email addresses are also easy for a business to verify, and, depending on the company's user-authentication rules, offer the added advantage that the customer does not need to remember yet another unique password. If an email address 'bounces', it is relatively easy to request the user to update it during a return visit. Furthermore, an email address is often captured in an organisation's non-Internet systems, so it allows existing customers to be identified during the registration process.

User authentication, using either email addresses or some other code, is the best way to identify who is accessing your website. Users who are engaged with your site, not simply surfing the net or passing time, will be prepared to provide you with this information and to let you know that they are visiting.

However, there are other methods available for the collection of information about your website audience. These methods produce data of varying degrees of richness and accuracy. Some of these methods can complement the user-authentication method, but none of them produces information as rich as that collected from a registration process.

Cookies

Some websites use cookies to identify visitors to the site. Cookies are small packets of data that are deposited on the computer hard disk of the user when that person visits a site. Cookies can contain all sorts of information, such as the visitor's unique identification number for that site, the last time that person visited the site, the visitor's ISP location, and so on. Figure 9.1 (page 164) gives a few examples of what cookies look like.

Figure 9.1 looks a lot like cryptology, doesn't it? However, a few recognisable elements do appear—such as page URLs, IP addresses, and webserver names. Also note that some websites create multiple cookies. For example, the second and third cookies from excite.com have a common number in them, which the website is apparently using to identify that it is the same user.

Different browsers handle cookies in different ways. On PCs using Netscape, for example, the information is put into a file called 'cookies.txt' and each new cookie writes a single line in this file. Microsoft Internet Explorer, in contrast, stores each cookie in a separate file.

All of the cookies stored on the browsers are accessible to any page or script on the server that created the cookie. So when someone visits a site, the script asks for its cookie and, assuming there is one, can then look up the relevant profile

---

Figure 9.1 Cookie examples

LookSmartPIN 000722x6818bdd1015ae2a8dd1,isp=OZ,Ped looksmart.com.au/ 0 3180909312 30094053 661999200 29359800 *

Registered no excite.com/ 0 1073733632 30124258 3451966496 29359799 *

UID FE47CABE398BD016 excite.com/ 0 1073733632 30124258 3451966496 29359799 *

ORA_UID SEARCH_2255227 www.oracle.com/pls/intermedia/ 0 1573113600 29452150 4079589696 29378724 *

SITESERVER ID=a0ce0cb4e4b74b61260074240097dff3 buynow.com/ 0 642859008 31887777 3937976224 29382506 *

SITESERVER ID=a5cebb1e359a9d8463ff22c054998a63 deloitte.com/ 0 642859008 31887777 1812965248 29345712 *

Apache 198.142.219.128.938095923236194 www.elance.com/ 0 1851406976 30079544 1262264160 29345290 *

Apache 198.142.216.37.18724980917168690 www.netratings.com/ 0 176373555229431988 3159623712 29395778 *

Apache 198.142.216.37.19076980915352462 www.nielsen.netratings.com/ 0 783604736 29431984 1994660192 29395773 *

---

information in its database. This might be personal information of a sensitive nature, such as credit card details or a delivery address. If there is no cookie for the website, the webserver creates the cookie and writes it to the new visitor's hard disk. During the visit, if the visitor undertakes more activities, the webserver might decide to change the cookie's content. E-commerce sites, for example, write into a visitor's cookie the names of items which that visitor puts into a shopping cart. In these circumstances, a script program deletes the old cookie and creates a new one. Some sites have cookies that expire when a user exits the site.

When some form of conversion takes place, this usually involves an exchange of information. This additional information can also be linked to the user's cookie.

The website currently being visited cannot read cookies that other sites have stored on the visitor's hard disk. However, an interesting situation arises when websites source and display content from other sites, such as advertising, news feeds, and affiliate programs. In this situation a site other than the one being visited might create a cookie on the visitor's hard drive. Let us take the example of an online bookstore. If a user visits a news portal that is an affiliate of the bookstore, the online bookstore might create a cookie telling the bookstore that the user has visited the news portal. Similarly, if a user goes to a sports portal that is an affiliate of the bookstore, the bookstore might also know that the user has visited the sports site. Unless users have read the privacy statement of the online bookstore, the users will probably remain unaware that the bookstore can track them as they visit their affiliate sites.

There are several problems with cookies, and website operators should be wary of using them as the only means of identifying customers. These problems include:

- users who set their browser to prevent cookies being created on their hard disks;
- users who delete cookies as part of cleaning their temporary files;
- visitors who use multiple machines and devices to access a single website; and
- multiple users who share a single computer to access the same website.

The first problem (users preventing cookies) arises from the common misconception that cookies are insecure. This is incorrect. There is no security issue involved with cookies. Cookies are the only files that browsers can create on a user's hard disk, and they cannot create, delete, or alter any other type of file. Moreover, a cookie created by a webserver can be accessed and manipulated only by that webserver. Although some people might see cookies as representing an invasion of privacy, cookies can also make things easier for the user by remembering that person's user identification and password, and other preferences and profile data.

The second problem (users deleting cookies) arises when the user chooses to clean up his or her temporary files. Certain operating systems try to discourage users from accessing any files under the systems directory, but many people still do it. If this happens, when that person goes to a previously visited website, it will treat the person as a new user, and the user will not benefit from any personalisation that the site is capable of, based on the information in the user's cookie file. This is a serious issue for websites that rely solely on cookies to identify their visitors. However, if the website has a registration-based user authentication, the site can create a new cookie for the user upon that person's next visit.

The third problem (multiple machines and devices) arises from mobility. Mobility is a fact of life today. People access the Internet from a variety of locations, using different machines and devices to visit the same site. If cookies are the only means of identifying a visitor, the website will create a new identity for a particular person at each access point. The problem is overcome if the site uses a registration-based authentication method in addition to using cookies.

The fourth problem (multiple users from a single machine) differs from the others, and applies when several people use the same computer to access your website. Think of a family with one PC shared among all members of the family. As each family member accesses the same site, the website will 'think' that each person is the same user, and will keep building on the one profile. Some websites have developed functionality to avoid this situation and ask the user to confirm his or her identity. Amazon.com is a good example of this. When a user visits Amazon's homepage, the user receives a message in large letters asking the person to confirm his or her identity.

So cookies have problems. From the above discussion it is obvious that using cookies as the only way of identifying users will produce misleading results. In many instances, cookies will save your visitors time, as they do not have to identify themselves every time they visit. Cookies are also useful to website owners as an easy form of identification, offering the possibility of providing a more personalised service. However, they are not sufficient on their own, and result in better outcomes if used in conjunction with other methods of user authentication.

IP addresses

Every computer connected to the Internet is assigned an IP address or Internet protocol number. This enables other computers on the Internet to know where requests are coming from and where information should be sent to. At a glance, IP addresses seem to be an ideal measure for user identification, because the webservers can record them and thus know when a user visits again. However, there are significant issues with this technique.

First, dial-up users are not assigned a permanent IP address. Every time such a user connects to the Internet, that person's Internet service provider (ISP) assigns a temporary IP address. Therefore, even if the same user visits a website on two consecutive days, it is more than likely that a different IP address will be used on each occasion. This is a significant issue considering the large number of dial-up users—as noted previously, according to Jupiter Communication, 80 per cent of users will still be reaching the Internet through dial-up modems in 2002.[1]

Second, ISPs might use a small number of public IP addresses (or perhaps only one) to communicate with the Internet, making it extremely difficult for the webservers to recognise different users. When a user makes a request to view a website, the request is sent in packets to the ISP. These packets contain the temporary IP address assigned to the user by the ISP. The ISP resolves these packets and might change the send-from address in the IP packet to one of its own public IP addresses before sending it on to the webserver hosting the website. This process can cause webservers to 'think' they are receiving requests from many users through the one IP address, or through the IP address of the proxy server through which the users are making the request, as opposed to the IP address of the user making the request. Some large ISPs, such as AOL, might send *all* requests by its users via the one IP address.

Finally, firewalls are used by system administrators to increase the security of networks. Accessing the Internet through a firewall does not allow the webserver log file to record a unique IP address. Instead, a general IP address is recorded. This creates a difficult problem for sites that rely on IP addresses to identify users—every user who requests a page through the one firewall will have the same IP address.

It is apparent that IP addresses collected by webserver log files are inadequate for identifying users. If the user-activity data are collected at the webserver level, you should not use IP addresses, unless this is the only technique available.

Combining user-identification techniques

As illustrated above, all user-identification techniques produce results with varying degrees of richness and accuracy. To achieve greater accuracy, organisations can use a combination of user-identification techniques. The choice of

---

CASE STUDY
Stinger's Online Cars
Combining user-identification techniques

Stinger's Online Cars can use a cookie-based identification system for a customer who is in the *acquire* stage. By doing this, Stinger can track the number of times the customer visits the site before engaging in any of *conversion* activities, such as booking a test drive. To book the test drive, the customer has to provide more specific personal details. At this stage, Stinger can link the cookie information and the personal details of the customer to recognise any repeat visits.

If the customer purchases a vehicle, and is set up at the website as a 'vehicle owner' (so he or she can access information on maintenance, service, or financial information), this person should be assigned a secure registration number.

Throughout the customer-engagement process, Stinger can use multiple user-identification techniques—depending on the stage that the customer has reached.

techniques might change during different stages of engagement with the user, as the organisation collects more knowledge of the user's identity, needs, and online behaviour patterns.

COLLECTING USER-ACTIVITY DATA

This section on collecting user-activity data considers:

- server-based measurement;
- browser-based measurement;
- network-based measurement; and
- implications of broadband access for user-activity data.

Server-based measurement—data collection from webservers

The webserver is the first port of call for measurement practices, because every user interacts with these, regardless of what he or she is trying to achieve. In other words, each website requires a webserver to respond to user requests—whether it is a brochure-ware site or an advanced business application. Web-servers are therefore the most researched source of data in terms of measurement.

All webservers record interaction details into one or more log files or databases. These log files are used to monitor the server's technical performance, record unauthorised requests, and provide server-activity information. Many of the website analytical tools available today rely on this server-activity information to produce traffic and behavioural information about the users of a website. This section focuses on measurements performed on this activity information, which is known as *server-based measurement*.

Most webservers adopt a CERN/NCSA common log format (CLG or CLOG), which means that their logs are formatted in the same way as the CERN and NCSA servers.[2] Data elements suggested by CLG include: client IP address; client user ID (rarely used); client user name (rarely used); date and time; request; status of the request; and bytes served. Two additional data elements were added in the extended common log file format (ECLF)—referrer and user agent.

Before providing definitions of these data elements, some of the differences introduced by webserver vendors should be addressed.

■ The sequence of data elements and their labels can change from one web-server to the next, and it is possible to use one of several predefined formats, or to specify a custom format.

■ Some webservers keep many logs (for example, error logs). Others allow the same information to be written into different formats, with the formats often being defined by the system administrator. Others allow for different logs for different kind of actions.

■ The meaning of data elements can vary slightly. It is therefore advisable to refer to the administration manuals provided by the vendor of the webserver.

■ Webservers add additional data elements to the log files. CGI scripts can enter information (such as security alerts or abnormal user requests) into the log. Servers can create 'non-hit' log entries (such as comments). Particular events (for example, time passing or the server load exceeding a certain limit) can also generate entries in the log. Some of these are becoming more popular and are accepted data elements. They are therefore included in the discussion below. However, it is important to note that the scope of extending the data elements is inevitably limited to the information contained in the HTTP protocol.

Log files are usually flat files, and data elements are recorded with space delimiters. Typically, webservers use a minus sign to indicate that a data element is not applicable or cannot be determined. The web administrator can specify that new logs be started on a regular basis (normally each day) and that old logs be archived for review. If this feature is not available, log files can become very large and unmanageable. The archived log files can be sent into real-time applications using the webserver's common gateway interface (CGI), which enables the web administrator to import log files into one of the many log-file analysis programs available on the market.

Figure 9.2 (opposite) shows a log file with some sample records (truncated for presentation here).

Table 9.1 (page 172) provides examples of some of the data elements that appear in Figure 9.2.

Figure 9.2 A few lines of a typical log file

2001-05-18 00:21:15 203.147.239.77 POST /Default.asp - 302 0 409 588 1642 80 HTTP/1.1

2001-05-18 00:21:17 203.147.239.77 GET /styles.css - 304 0 143 427 0 80 HTTP/1.1

2001-05-18 00:21:27 203.147.239.77 GET /default2.asp - 200 0 95911 456 11867 80

2001-05-18 00:21:46 203.147.239.77 GET /g_main.shtm - 200 0 22238 468 991 80 HTTP/1.1

2001-05-18 00:22:00 203.147.239.77 GET /g_list.asp TermTitle=B 200 0 41082 478 4065 80

2001-05-18 00:22:09 203.147.239.77 GET /g_add.asp - 200 0 8010 476 942 80 HTTP/1.1

2001-05-18 00:22:39 203.147.239.77 POST /g_add.asp - 302 0 447 932 2494 80 HTTP/1.1

2001-05-18 00:22:41 203.147.239.77 GET /styles.css - 304 0 143 437 0 80 HTTP/1.1

2001-2001-05-18 00:23:30 203.147.239.77 GET /g_list.asp TermTitle=W 200 0 31080 489 1893 80

2001-05-18 00:23:34 203.147.239.77 GET /g_add.asp - 200 0 8010 476 311 80 HTTP/1.1

2001-05-18 00:23:55 203.147.239.77 POST /g_add.asp - 302 0 447 665 160 80 HTTP/1.1

2001-05-18 00:23:57 203.147.239.77 GET /styles.css - 304 0 143 437 0 80 HTTP/1.1

2001-05-18 00:23:57 203.147.239.77 GET /confirm_contribute.htm - 200 0 16520 476 1532

2001-05-18 00:24:07 192.11.223.116 GET /industry.asp SegmentId=29 302 0 309 477 3094

2001-05-18 00:24:07 192.11.223.116 GET /loginrequired.asp - 200 0 7147 166 80 80

Table 9.1 Webserver log record, examples of data elements

Data Element	Example
Date time	2001-05-18 00:22:00
Client IP address	198.142.217.77
User ID	—
User name	—
Server IP address	203.147.239.77
Server port	80
Request	Combination of method, filename, and query
Method	GET
Filename	/g_list.asp
Query	TermTitle=B
Status	200
Bytes	478
Time taken	4065
User agent	Mozilla/4.0+(compatible;+MSIE+5.5;+Windows+98)
Referrer	http://www.ebusinessresourcecenter.com/q_main.shtm
Cookie	ASPSESSIONIDGQQGGHVC=DKMMIEJAHGGMKJNC DHDCMBMK

Definitions of webserver log file data elements

Definitions of the data elements shown in Table 9.1 are presented below, together with some thoughts on how each of them can be used for website analysis.

Date time

Date time is usually the date and time that a request is successfully completed. Your server specifications will indicate exactly what time is logged.

Client IP address

The *client IP address* is the Internet address of the browser or the other agent making the request, and is the address to which the server's response will be sent. Most webservers have the ability to resolve this address into a text domain name using an Internet query protocol called 'reverse address lookup'.

Considering the large volume of log files, this increases the load on the web-server. It is more reasonable to expect to resolve IP addresses into domain names with website analytical tools.

User ID
The *user ID* is the remote log-in name of the user. This is an arbitrary identifier supplied by web browsers using a protocol called 'web daemon'. This authentication technique is seldom used by web browsers. A minus sign is typically placed in the field.

User name
The *user name* is the name by which the user authenticated himself or herself using a password protected page via the HTTP secure sockets layer (SSL). This field will be filled in only if the user has correctly identified himself or herself, otherwise a minus sign is typically placed in the field.

Server IP address
The *server IP address* is the IP address of the website being accessed. If all the components of a website are served from the same webserver, this data element shows the same IP address for all requests in the log file. Composite or mirrored websites show different IP addresses, which might log into the same or separate log files.

Server port
The *server port* is the number of the TCP/IP port on a host, which has served the logged activity. It is standard web practice to reserve port 80 for an HTTP server and port 443 to a secure HTTP server using SSL.

Request
A *request* is the exact request line as it came from the browser. It contains method, filename, and query (see below).

Method
The *method* is the method used to retrieve the page—typically GET or POST. GET requests an object from the webserver whereas POST sends information from browser to webserver.

Filename

The *filename* is the name or the uniform resource identifier (URI) of the object being requested. It is expressed either as a full path or relative path to the homepage. For example, /default.asp shows a relative path.

Query

The *query* is the URI of the query that is required to display the object being requested. Query strings are often used for dynamic pages. Examples include SegmentId=29 *or* TermTitle=B.

Status

The *status* is a 3-digit HTTP response code returned to the client. It indicates whether the file was successfully retrieved, and, if not, what error message has occurred. Table 9.2 (below) shows the significance of the first letters used in the error codes.

Table 9.3 (opposite) provides a list of commonly used status codes and their definitions. The webservers have similar codes but their meanings might vary somewhat. It is advisable to refer to the server administration manuals for full definitions.

Table 9.2 Meaning of first letters of status codes		
Code	**Type**	**Meaning**
1XX	Informational	The HTTP 1.0 protocol does not use informational response codes. Therefore, there are no 1XX series responses.
2XX	Success	The request was received, understood, and served.
3XX	Redirection	Further action is required to complete the request.
4XX	Client error	The request contains bad syntax and cannot be fulfilled.
5XX	Server error	The server failed to fulfil an apparently valid request.

Table 9.3 Commonly used status codes

Code	Definition	Code	Definition
100	Continue	405	Method not allowed
101	Switching protocols	406	Not accepted
200	OK	407	Proxy authentication
201	Created		required
202	Accepted	408	Request time-out
204	No content	410	Gone
205	Reset content	411	Length required
206	Partial content	412	Precondition failed
300	Multiple choices	413	Request entity too large
301	Moved permanently	414	Request URI too large
302	Moved temporarily	425	Unsupported media type
303	See other	500	Internal server error
304	Not modified	501	Not implemented
305	Use proxy	502	Bad gateway
400	Bad request	503	Service unavailable
401	Unauthorised	504	Gateway time-out
402	Payment required	505	HTTP version not
403	Forbidden		supported
404	Not found		

Bytes

Bytes refers to the number of bytes transferred to the client.

Time taken

The *time taken* refers to the time in seconds to serve the request from the web-server. This data element is useful in monitoring server performance.

User agent

The *user agent* is the name and version of the client software making the request, and the operating system that the client uses. This data element can help determine which features to use in webpage design, such as Dynamic HTML or JavaScript. Alternatively serverpages can use it to identify the browser type, and then display only features that are supported by that browser.

Referrer

The *referrer* is a text string that can be sent by the client to indicate the original source of a request or link. It provides the exact path (or URL) of where the user clicked on a link to arrive at your site, and is therefore a useful data element to monitor how often links provided at other sites are used.

Cookie

This contains the unique user identifier that identifies the user to the website. The mechanics of how cookies work is discussed in detail as part of user-identification techniques. (See page 163.)

How does server-based measurement work?

Log files created by webservers can be used to measure user-activity data, perform analysis, and create reports on website traffic. There is a rapidly growing market that offers tools and services for this purpose. The reports usually contain information about user activity, but the capabilities are often limited to a standard set of reports which cannot be customised to measure your site's specific metrics. As discussed in Chapter 1 (page 5), these standard metrics and reports have little value and can be misleading.

> Visit <www.hurolinan.com> to read the reviews of *server-based measurement solution providers* [Locator Code 105].

If you are hosting your website at an ISP, it is likely that the ISP will provide you with a website-traffic analytical tool that uses webserver log files. Note that the ISP might charge you extra for supplying these base data.

Issues with served-based measurement

People who are opposed to using server log files argue that webserver log files were created to troubleshoot webserver performance, not to drive marketing and business decisions.

Webserver log files are unaware of the visits that are served from caching— of whatever type. In these cases the log files will not record the activity at all, and final figures will therefore be less than the actual figures of usage.

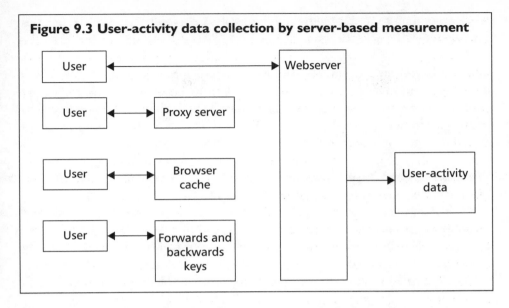

Figure 9.3 User-activity data collection by server-based measurement

Figure 9.3 (above) shows that webserver log files will not log activities when the requests are met by caches at proxy servers, browsers, and backwards and forwards keys.

If comprehensive research on the magnitude of caching exists, it is difficult to find. According to vendors, browser caching and proxy-server caching accounts for 10—30 per cent of the overall traffic. Websites that contain only static pages are affected by caching more than websites in which content is dynamically served from a database. This is because the webpage, to display the content, needs to perform a query while the page is being served, and the webserver will record this user activity.

Another issue with webserver log files is that they capture activity details at a more granular level than that required to measure and analyse the websites. Webserver log files create a new record for each component of a webpage, including pictures, frames, and so on. It is necessary to strip out these data before reporting the metric results.

Finally, server log files not only record activities requested by real users but also record activities requested by machines (such as robots). These activities should be cleansed before reporting the metric results. Chapter 10 (page 191) includes a more detailed discussion on robots.

Browser-based measurement—an alternative to server log files

It is possible to measure user activities at the browser level, and this technique addresses some of the shortfalls of server-based measurement. If you choose to use this technique, it is important to understand what it involves, why you would consider it, how it is implemented, and the implications of its use.

What is browser-based measurement?

Browser-based measurement allows web activity to be measured at the user's personal computer. It measures the number of times a browser loads a page and its contents—regardless of whether it is cached or not. Unlike server-based measurement, with browser-based measurement you can measure the activity resulting from the pages that are received from cache resources including a proxy server, PC cache, or backwards and forwards keys (see Figure 9.4 opposite).

Why consider browser-based measurement?

Browser-based measurement addresses the following shortfalls of webserver log files in collecting user-activity data:

▮ reduces undercounting caused by page-caching;
▮ eliminates overcounting caused by robots (webcrawlers and agents);
▮ collects more accurate IP address from behind firewalls; and
▮ eliminates the extensive data-cleansing required for server-based measurement because it records only real-user activities at the page level.

Performance is a big issue on the Internet. To improve performance, and thus enhance user experience, various caching techniques are used. These might be at the proxy server, PC, and/or browser levels.

Proxy servers are used within networks to manage traffic load. They hold copies of prerequested files so that users receive files from the fastest, most efficient source. Popular webpages can be cached on literally thousands of proxy servers around the world. It is claimed that some ISPs cache up to 80 per cent of their most popular files.

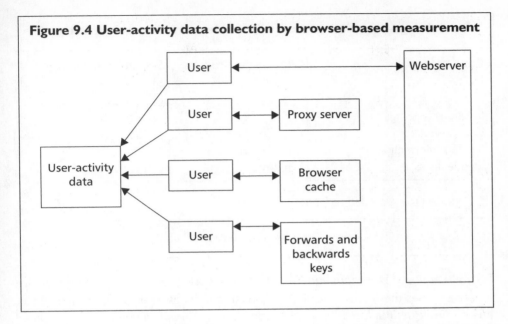

Figure 9.4 User-activity data collection by browser-based measurement

Similarly, browsers store webpages on a PC's hard disk. When a user requests a webpage, the browser first checks the PC cache to see if a copy is on hand. If so, the browser delivers the page from the hard disk, rather than via the Internet. This improves the speed of page-loading and reduces network congestion. Obviously this activity is not recorded on the webserver's log file, as the request was never made to the Internet.

When a user hits the backwards or forwards keys on the browser, the pages are held in RAM. Again this page request is not recorded on the server log file because the request has not been made to the Internet.

Table 9.4 (page 180) illustrates the differences in browser-based and server-based measurement from the same set of activities on the website of a vendor who promotes browser-based measurement.

Because browser-based measurement requires a page to be fully loaded on a browser, this technique will not count automated programs (such as webcrawlers, robots, and spiders) that artificially increase site activity.

Table 9.4 Page-view timings from client-side and server-side tracking		
Page title	**Client-side timings**	**Server-side timings**
Home	11h 1m 56s	11h 1m 56s
Company information	11h 6m 20s	11h 6m 20s
Solutions	11h 6m 24s	11h 6m 19s
Demonstration	11h 25m 14s*	11h 25m 32s*
Contact information	11h 0m 30s*	11h 0m 24s*
Frequently asked questions	11h 2m 29s*	11h 2m 23s*
* Denotes time recorded so far for current page		
Source: Clickstream Technology plc. See www.clickstream.com.		

Firewalls are used by system administrators to increase the security of a network. If a user accesses the Internet through a firewall, the webserver log file is unable to record a unique IP address. Instead, a general IP address is recorded. This creates a big issue for sites that rely on IP addresses for identifying users because different users requesting pages through the same firewall will have the same IP address.

How does browser-based measurement work?

Websites using browser-based measurement insert a script program into every webpage of the site. When the page is loaded into a browser, this program sends the details of the activity to a central collection machine, which records the activity in the log file. There are several vendors that focus solely on browser-based measurement.

Visit <www.hurolinan.com> to read the reviews of *browser-based measurement service providers* [Locator Code 106].

Implications of browser-based measurement

There are several issues associated with browser-based measurement. It is important to be aware of these so you can decide which approach is more suitable for your requirements, and can ask the right questions when looking for a prospective vendor.

Your website might have performance issues as a result of adding scripts that were developed in-house. By using a third-party service provider, whose scripts are generally refined and tested for optimum performance, you can avoid such problems.

Pages served from behind a firewall, or by browsers that block all Java transmissions, cannot be measured via Java-based program scripts. In these instances, your script needs to switch to an alternative script (such as CGI) as the collection mechanism. Although there is no formal research that quantifies how often this situation occurs, it is generally not believed to be statistically significant. As more and more websites use Java-based components, security concerns associated with Java transmissions are expected to reduce over time.

For Java Applet-based programs, when the user visits the site for the first time, the browser needs to download the class library of the Java Applet into the PC. As this happens only on their first visit, and has minimal impact on performance, it is not believed to be a significant issue.

Finally, as the name implies, this technique of data collection requires a browser to be used as the access method to the website. Access to the Internet is not confined to browsers, and more and more alternative Internet devices are entering the market. These devices often have less performance capacity than PCs, and it is much less feasible to use this approach. Server log files, in contrast, do capture the activity of these devices, as well as that of web browsers.

Network-based measurement

Server-based and browser-based measurement techniques focus on collecting user-activity data from websites. As mobile commerce, Internet devices, and Internet protocols other than HTTP—such as chat, email, instant messaging, and file transfer (FTP)—become ubiquitous, these two techniques become insufficient to capture all of the user-activity data. A host of vendors are addressing this limitation by developing techniques that will encompass not only websites but also any other applications that use the Internet.

One of these techniques is *network-based measurement*, whereby user-activity data are collected from the network by deciphering the content of data packets as they move across the network. This is also called 'packet sniffing'. This is not a new technique—it has been used for network administration and management purposes for many years.

Network measurement can be best done at Internet service provider (ISP) level. ISPs have a 'bird's-eye view' of all web-user activities. In selecting vendors from this category, keep in mind that a close match should be sought between the demographics of the website and that of the area served by the ISP. Ensure that the vendor's arrangements with the ISP preserve this compatibility of demographics.

Visit <www.hurolinan.com> to read the reviews of *network-based measurement service providers* [Locator Code 107].

If the scope of your eBusiness initiative goes beyond a traditional website, your data-collection strategies should reflect this, and allow for the fact that servers that handle the requests for Internet devices are different from webservers. Wireless applications, for example, are served by wireless servers that employ a completely different protocol from HTTP. For one of these protocols, wireless application protocol (WAP), requests are transmitted to telecommunication companies with WAP gateways, where they are then translated and sent to wireless servers. The results are served with wireless markup language (WML). WAP protocol does not use IP addresses. It uses device-level identification to serve the content—such as the SIM card of a mobile phone. With 3G, (third generation technology) each device has a permanent IP address. Another popular wireless protocol is iMode, which is commonly used in Japan at present, and expected to spread to other countries.

The nature and richness of user-activity data from Internet devices differ from those of websites. Internet devices usually have significantly smaller user interfaces, so content must be cut into elementary pieces that are sufficient for users to make sense of, and make decisions. The absence of a mouse, large graphics, and large emails differentiates these devices. Furthermore, you cannot use client scripting or cookies for user identification.

The above discussion, although brief, highlights the need to consider the impact of Internet devices, and therefore other Internet protocols, when measuring the overall success of your organisation's online initiatives.

Implications of broadband access for user-activity data

Broadband offers users permanent connection to the Internet with a significantly larger bandwidth than that of dial-up access. This means that every device connected to the Internet via broadband is assigned a permanent and unique IP address. This seems like good news for web measurement because it will facilitate user identification. However, universal broadband access is still a long way off, and therefore the other methods previously discussed might still be more favourable for user identification.

Broadband users are likely to consume more web content and have less issues with page load-times. This discounts the importance of website-performance efficiency measures.

In addition, broadband is likely to increase the usage of protocols other than HTTP, such as chat. The business use of these protocols can open up new opportunities, and you need to consider data-collection methodologies for these protocols that are founded upon a common strategy. With broadband using other protocols, servers can leave more than a cookie at the client machine when non browser-based protocols are used.

MINDING THE PRIVACY OF USERS

To get to know your customers better, and thus serve their needs more adequately, it is obvious that you need to collect personal data about them and their activities on your website.

The ethics of unauthorised acquisition and use of personal information is a strongly debated issue. Research firms have been investigating customer attitudes to this through surveys. Privacy advocates have been lobbying governments to introduce legislation protecting the privacy of individuals with regard to their online behaviour. Many law cases have been initiated by corporations and individuals claiming that their privacy has been breached. Not surprisingly, many software companies are trying to make money out of the situation by releasing solutions and services that promise privacy protection.

In an alarming case, an Internet advertisement-placement agency, Double-Click, which had thousands of high-profile clients, hit the headlines for cross-referencing offline and online data. The company's software linked information gathered from offline sources (such as names and addresses) with online information (such as email addresses, websites frequented, and advertisements clicked on). There was a loud outcry and a court battle ensued. DoubleClick reined in its activities, although this sort of battle is far from over. The implications of this case for the future of privacy issues will be interesting to follow.

The most effective way to avoid privacy issues on your website is to ensure that your practices of data collection and usage are transparent to your users, and that you give them the option to refuse to participate.

The practices adopted by your organisation must comply with any legislation applicable in your country, and any legislation applicable in the countries of your target audiences. Cross-country legislation is a difficult area to negotiate, because there are still major differences in the extent and maturity of legislation in each country. If you are not able to meet the requirements of certain countries, but still want these people to use your online services, you must clearly state your position in your privacy policy.

Future of privacy
There are many parallels between an organisation's approach to privacy and its approach to other responsibilities that it has to the wider community. Protocols for appropriate ethical behaviour are now common in many aspects of business. It is therefore likely that a number of generally accepted privacy practices will develop, and that companies will seek compliance audits:

■ to convince themselves and their stakeholders that they are not breaching what they are preaching; and
■ to provide proof of their compliance to website users.

However, there is still a long way to go before a balance is attained between the needs of organisations and the desires of users. Eventually, common practices will be able to protect individual privacy while giving organisations enough intelligence to allow them to understand and relate to the needs of their customers.

What can we do now?

A good starting-point is to examine some of the many privacy principles suggested by industry organisations, and select one that suits the needs of both your users and your business. As an example, the Interactive Advertising Bureau (IAB) provides guidelines that are enforceable on their members. The IAB recommends that a privacy policy must clearly state the following:

■ the information being collected and the purpose of its collection;

■ all methods of information collection used (such as a registration process, sweepstakes, and/or a feedback form);

■ the use of that information, and how the organisation will use the pii (personal identifiable information) collected for future marketing to the individual;

■ any possible third-party distribution of that information and, in the event that information is being disclosed to third parties, the policy making reference to which information is disclosed, why this disclosure takes place, and the relationship of the organisation to the third party;

■ the choices available to an individual regarding collection, the use and distribution of the collected information, and how to exercise these choices;

■ the consequences, if any, of an individual's refusal to provide information;

■ what steps the organisation takes to ensure data quality and access;

■ a statement of the organisation's commitment to data security;

■ whether the organisation supplements the pii (as collected) with their own data or information (as sourced from third parties), including the use of aggregated data (an example of this being the use of third party-acquired demographic or marketing data);

■ what accountability mechanisms the organisation uses (examples of this being measures such as internal or external reviews, or privacy audits that the organisation takes to assure compliance with their privacy policy); and

■ how and whom to contact within the organisation with any privacy-related questions or concerns.

The IAB also suggests that all sites that use a third-party ad server should provide information regarding the privacy policy and practices of that third-party ad server. This should be done via a link to that company's privacy policy page, and it should adhere to the IAB's forthcoming Online Privacy Alliance (OPA) and Network Advertising Initiative (NAI) guidelines.[3]

SUMMARY

The collation of user identities is the primary mechanism of gathering data required for measurement and, although such identities do not necessarily imply knowledge of a user's name and address, they do offer the ability to distinguish between the activities of different users.

There are several techniques that help identify users of a website, and they produce results of varying richness and accuracy. These techniques are as explicit as registration-based identification, or as implicit as the IP address used by the user in accessing the website. Organisations can combine a combination of user-identification techniques to achieve greater accuracy, and the choice of techniques might change during different stages of engagement with the user. This helps to build on existing knowledge of who the users are, what their needs are, and what online behaviour patterns they exhibit.

User-activity data can be captured at three distinct points—webserver, browser, or network. Each data-collection point has implications for measurement results, and involves different levels of complexity. The greatest criticism of server-based measurement is that log files were originally designed to measure the performance of websites, rather than user activities on these websites. Issues with this method (such as overcounting because of the requests of robots and spiders, undercounting due to extensive caching, and the need for cleansing of data due to the granular level of data captured at server log files) has led to the creation of another vendor market segment, which collects user-activity data at browser level. This technique requires insertion of a code into every page of a website. There are several issues with this, such as the compromising of per-formance due to additional code, and the difficulty of importing the code into Internet devices. More recently, vendors have developed solutions that can capture user-activity data at network level. This technique has good prospects because it addresses some of the issues of concern that exist with the other two techniques, and because it is suitable for collecting data from Internet protocols other than HTTP.

The ethics of the unauthorised acquisition and use of personal information is a heavily debated topic. The practices adopted by your organisation must comply with all legislation applicable to the countries of target users. Organisations must understand the privacy issues and must implement transparent privacy practices to convince the users, themselves, and their stakeholders that there is no breach of personal privacy. Third-party privacy compliance audits might be suitable for certain websites, because they offer a greater level of comfort to users during their interactions with your website.

CHAPTER

10

**Preparing the Data
for Anaylsis**

Cleansing user-activity data—removing the elements that do not qualify for measurement, and integrating and consolidating the remainder with data collected from other sources—is a challenge. But it is crucial to the establishment of a meaningful representation of what is happening with an online initiative.

This chapter stresses the importance of using consistent data of quality to produce meaningful results. In doing so, the chapter advocates the removal of various types of non-qualifying user-activity data. It also defines which other data elements—from offline sources, and from other online sources—might be required to integrate and consolidate with user-activity data, and provides a checklist for conducting this task. Finally, the chapter advises on how to deal with large volumes of data.

CLEANSING USER-ACTIVITY DATA

Many activities that occur on your website need to be identified as non-qualifying user-activity data, because they are additional to genuine user-activity data generated by real users. If captured by the log files that are used for measurement, these activities should be excluded. Failure to do so will create skewed results.

These non-qualifying data-generating activities include:

■ internal site-management and maintenance activities;
■ documents embedded in pages;
■ unsuccessful server requests;
■ navigational elements;
■ robots;
■ server-pushed pages;
■ page-refreshes; and
■ serving content from other websites.

This is not an exhaustive list. As technology evolves, more non-qualifying activities could emerge, and the decision to include or exclude them in your analysis should be made on a case-by-case basis. When you produce your measurement reports, it is strongly recommended that you include an explanatory note clearly stating which activities are included in the analysis. This is especially important for reports that are produced for external purposes.

If your company chooses to use the services of a web-traffic measurement company or a website audit company, its report is likely to exclude many, if not all, of these non-qualifying activities from the results.

Notes on each of these non-qualifying data-generating activities follow.

Internal site-management and maintenance activities

Internal activity generated as a result of site management and maintenance should not qualify for inclusion in your analysis. It can be rejected by looking up the machine's IP address or host name. However, normal activity generated by employees of the website might be considered valid. To distinguish between valid and invalid internal activity, it is necessary to identify all internal IP addresses, host names, or URLs for management and maintenance of webpages.

Documents embedded in pages

Webservers create a record in the log file for each document that has been requested from a site, and this includes the *documents embedded in pages*. Although it might be important for you to measure how well these documents download, unless activity within a page is being analysed these should be excluded from overall analysis. The filter rule is based on the file extension or MIME type (type of file that was requested). Common MIME types include text/HTML, image/gif, image/jpg, and video/mpg.

Unsuccessful server requests

Webservers capture and record the status code of requests. These are 3-digit codes that can be used to determine *whether the server successfully fulfilled* a specific request. ABC Interactive, an American website audit firm, suggests that valid status codes include 200 (for 'OK'), 201 (for 'created'), 202 (for 'accepted'), 203 (for 'non-authoritative information'), and 304 (for 'not modified').

The definitions of the codes are taken from the Apache Server, and other webservers might have similar codes with slightly different meanings. You must be careful when analysing the status codes—although they represent a mechanical activity, their meaning to you might vary from the above definitions. Take the example of status code 206, which represents 'partial content'. This might well be a successful request by the user, because he or she might have clicked on another link before the page had fully downloaded. This activity should be counted if the user went to another page at the site, but not counted if that person exited the site—although this distinction could be tricky to capture.

Navigational elements

Including *navigational items* (such as frames and 'file includes') skew total page-views in the analysis. These should be identified and removed to avoid double counting.

These days, navigational items are a standard part of any website. Frames permit the simultaneous display of multiple documents within a browser window, and they are laid out as per instructions from the main file or frame holder. Additional files are utilised for each of the panels in the frame and the content portion of the page.

Unfortunately, most access logs contain one record for the frame holder and an additional one for every panel on the screen. According to standard definition, the entire document translates into one page-view regardless of the number of panels displayed in the document. Therefore, only the content page should be considered a valid record. To avoid double counting, the URLs of documents other than the content page should be identified and eliminated from the analysis.

Robots

Various types of *robots* visit websites. Their activity should be considered as non-qualifying, because user-activity data should consist of only the requests made to a website by real people.

Robots are used for various purposes. For example, search engines often use them to update their listings by indexing websites, individual users use them in downloading content to read offline, or a site might use them (in the form of monitoring software) to ensure that the site is operational.

Two common types of robots are spiders and agents. Spiders, or webcrawlers, traverse the hypertext structure by retrieving a document and then recursively retrieving all other documents that are referenced. They can start from almost anywhere on the web, and will keep moving to new links as they come across them. They receive their name from the way in which they 'crawl' the web, and they are commonly used by search engines. Agents, in contrast, visit a website to perform a specific task, such as finding the latest news and downloading it into a user's computer, or monitoring Internet traffic and reporting its usage.

It is often possible to detect robots. They usually identify themselves in the user-agent data element of webserver log files. The user-agent data elements can be checked against the list of agents available from many sources, such as ABC Interactive. Furthermore, you can create a robots.txt file to specify which robots are permitted to the site and whether they have complete access, limited access, or no access. Most robot programs will seek this file first and generally obey the rules set in it.

Server-pushed pages

Server-pushed pages are the pages that pop up without your consent in your browser when you are navigating around certain sites. Many sites use this technique for online surveys and marketing activities, and this is a useful tool for companies that have a particular message to push. Users who accommodate 'impulse activities' respond well to these.

You can create rules to determine whether these pages are displayed or not. These can be very simple, such as displaying the page on every person's browser, or on more targeted browsers. Regardless of the rule, however, server-pushed pages are not requested by the user, but are enforced on them.

Their inclusion in overall traffic measurement is debatable. If you use this technique, you need to measure how effective it is for you. However, if you use a web-measurement audit firm it might be inclined to disqualify server-pushed pages from its measurements.

Page-refreshes

Websites that offer dynamic content can automatically *refresh the page* after a certain time, which results in an artificial increase in page-views. This is a common technique used in discussion boards and chat applications. In these cases, the server writes a log record with the status code of 205, meaning 'reset content'.

Page-refreshes significantly skew the overall results and should be excluded from the analysis. You might even consider also removing user-initiated page-refreshes.

Serving content from other websites

Supplying content from external sources has become a common practice for many websites, because they realise the benefits of using third-party providers who can supply content with the same look and feel of the rest of the website. Unless the source of the content is explicitly stated, the user has no way of knowing that it has come from a third party. Note that this is different from the provision of links to external sites. Rather, this is the full display of the content without any links to the source, with the user not leaving the site.

Including or excluding such user activity served from external sources depends on how the organisation wants to account for this activity. However, you are strongly advised to treat the shared content separately.

INTEGRATING DATA FROM MULTIPLE SOURCES

Modern web applications do not stand alone. They need to integrate with other online and offline systems to provide better customer service and achieve transaction efficiencies.

When online applications are integrated with other systems, organisations need to put mechanisms in place so they can get an holistic view of customer and business activities. It is very likely that the metrics and analytical techniques will require data from multiple sources. These include:

❚ different sources of user-activity data for the same website;
❚ transactional data from operations systems;
❚ data from customer-interaction points; and
❚ data collected by external sources.

Each of these is considered below.

Different sources of user-activity data for the same website

As a website grows, *clusters* and *additional webservers* are used to heighten the performance of the site through load-balancing and other techniques. This means that pages are served from multiple webservers or from different clusters of the same webserver. In these circumstances, a user can view different pages from the same website via different clusters of a webserver or via entirely separate webservers. If you capture user-activity data at server level, each one of these server clusters and webservers will collect its own data, requiring consolidation to obtain full user-activity data.

Similarly, the operators of a website might choose to use *mirroring* to enhance site performance. Due to network loads, routers might direct requests to a mirror image of the website at another physical location to optimise the network traffic. A user can access the same website from a *mirrored* version of the site during a particular visit. However, during other visits, they might be accessing the original webserver. As a result, the user-activity data will be collected at multiple locations.

To consolidate the user-activity data from different sources, it is necessary to synchronise the timestamps in the log files. To achieve this, either the internal clocks of multiple servers must be completely synchronised or a time-translation map must be used. This is a challenge because even slight differences in the internal clocks will make the consolidation process very difficult, and can damage the quality of data.

Transactional data from operational systems

Many websites offer *transaction-based services* that integrate with other online and offline applications.

For example, a website with e-commerce functionality might accept an order from a customer. The customer might have chosen the order from a catalogue, which is uploaded from a product database at the enterprise resource planning (ERP) system. When the user places the order, the payment system validates the customer's credit card and informs the customer relationship management (CRM) system that it should email the customer to acknowledge the purchase. The order details are pushed into the ERP system for fulfilment. Once the order is packed and is ready to be shipped to the customer, the payment system debits the customer's credit card, the shipment system makes arrangements with the

---

CASE STUDY
Stinger's Online Cars
Integrating data from customer-interaction points

Stinger's Online Cars can gather customer data from its multiple websites, dealer networks, and other sources, and can organise these in a central repository.

The data from every interaction point with the customer—such as when car owners call about a loan or a new model—is captured and stored in the data warehouse to form the *customer knowledge system*. These data are accessible from all points in the company—including marketing executives, designers, finance managers, and executive managers.

---

freight company, and the CRM system informs the customer that the order is on its way and provides freight details.

Many of these activities take place outside the website. If a key goal of the organisation is operational excellence, one of the metrics it must monitor closely is the fulfilment lead-time. In this particular example, the details of these data reside in multiple systems—the website, ERP, CRM, payment, and shipment systems. To be able to measure this metric, the organisation must be able to capture the details of these data in a single repository, and must be able to integrate them.

Data from customer-interaction points
Your online channel is not the only *point of interaction with your customers*. For example, a person might browse your website for product and pricing information, and then choose to go to a physical store to purchase the product. This situation highlights the role that your website plays in lead-generation. It often shortens the conversion lead-time, because the customer is more informed when he or she visits your store and is therefore more qualified to make a decision.

There is significant evidence, supported by objective third-party research, that organisations able to integrate multiple channels can create a unified view of their customers. This is instrumental in realising business strategies faster and better. To establish a unified view of the customers, organisations should put in place processes that capture data from every customer-interaction point and store these in a single *customer knowledge system*.

Data collected by external sources

Other sources of data about the customers exist and might be utilised. These sources include flat files supplied in business-to-business relationships, third-party data from companies such as Dun & Bradstreet, and online polls or user surveys periodically conducted by organisations. If applicable to your organisation, these data can add new insights into the *customer knowledge system* if they are integrated with online user-activity data. These data can play a critical role in building repeat business with customers, permitting the continual refinement and targeting of marketing efforts.

Prerequisites for data integration

Two prerequisites for data integration are the *consistency* of the data and the *quality* of the data.

Consistency requires organisation-wide agreement on terminology and definitions. Data-cleansing activities, which were discussed above for web user-activity data (page 189), should also apply to data obtained from other sources.

Having data of good *quality* is one of the foundations of measurement. If you don't have such good-quality data, the measurement results will have little value.

Data-integration activities

To establish a *customer knowledge system* that provides a unified view of your customers, you should perform the following activities at a high level:

■ identify data-collection points in the organisation—start by looking at the customer-interaction points;
■ define unique identifiers for each data type and establish their relationships with other data sources;
■ define data-cleansing rules—be aware of data overlap and inconsistencies;
■ design processes to capture the data—make sure data collection is

embedded into operational processes, rather than being an after-thought; and

∎ integrate the data in a central location—such as a data warehouse.

DEALING WITH LARGE VOLUMES OF DATA

As organisations have increasingly used the Internet as a point of interaction with their customers, business partners, and employees, the volume of data generated—and therefore the volume of data requiring collection—has skyrocketed. It is estimated that busy websites such as Yahoo and Microsoft collect hundreds of gigabytes of user-activity data every day. Although most organisations will not be attracting the traffic that these large sites do, smaller organisations should still experience significant daily volumes of user-activity data. If organisations do not plan how to deal with such large volumes of data, the situation can become quite unmanageable, and valuable data can be wasted.

Organisations must start by examining the data sources available and checking these against business strategies to verify that they are useful for the business. At the same time, it is necessary to define how the data will be accessed and used. Once verified, systems should be put in place to collect and store the data in an efficient way. At the end of this activity, an organisation will have a clear data-collection strategy, which includes information that will determine the infra-structure required to handle the data. This infrastructure, at a high level, might include: (i) tools to extract, process, and load the data; (ii) a database or a data warehouse to store the data; and (iii) analytical tools to access, analyse, and report the data.

There are several other procedures that might help you deal with large volumes of data. These include:

∎ processing at the point of collection if possible;
∎ discarding non-qualifying data immediately;
∎ summarising data, where possible—if you are planning to store the data for future analysis, the summaries are often sufficient;
∎ questioning the value of storing each piece of data—if not properly used each data element can be a liability rather than an asset;
∎ making sure that data will be reused in the future; and

■ distinguishing between data that are required for real-time interaction with the client and data that must be stored for future measurement and reporting purposes.

SUMMARY

Defining a set of rules to identify and cleanse non-qualifying user-activity data is essential for meaningful metric results. The principle behind data-cleansing is the removal of all interactions with the website that do not originate from requests made by real users. These might include internal site-management and site-maintenance activities, documents embedded in pages, unsuccessful server requests, navigational elements (such as frames), the requests made by robots, server-pushed pages, page-refreshes, and serving content from other websites.

Web applications often integrate with other online and offline systems to provide better customer service and achieve transaction efficiencies. Organisations need to put in place mechanisms that enable a holistic view of the customer. This is achieved by using a *customer knowledge system*. This might require the integration of data from multiple sources—such as user-activity data from clustered and mirrored webservers, transactional data from operations systems, data from customer-interaction points, and data collected by external sources. Prerequisites for data integration and consolidation are the consistency and quality of data. Data collection should be embedded into the operational processes.

As organisations increasingly turn to the Internet as a viable customer-interaction tool, the volume of data collected has skyrocketed. Unless organisations put in place strategies to deal with these large volumes of data, the situation can become unmanageable and valuable data can go unrecorded.

Implementation of
Web Measurement

CHAPTER

11

**Resourcing Web
Measurement**

Web measurement is a serious task, and for any organisation that uses Internet technologies as an integral part of its business it is an enormous value-adding activity. Given its significance, web measurement should be a formal role assigned to a *web analyst*. Delegating this role among several people as a secondary task compromises the investment made in the online initiative and diminishes the likelihood of its success.

SKILLS REQUIREMENTS

Web analysts should be competent in many different areas. Analytical skills are the core competency, but web analysts should also have skills in human psychology, online marketing, business, and technology—as illustrated in Figure 11.1.

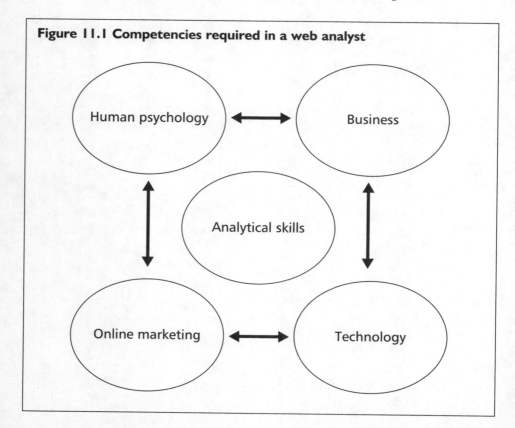

Figure 11.1 Competencies required in a web analyst

The importance of each of these competencies in a web analyst can be summarised as follows:

- analytical skills—to explore the data and discover patterns, meaningful relationships, anomalies, and trends;
- human psychology—to explain online behaviours, motivations, and frustrations;
- online marketing—to understand the purpose and contribution of marketing activities in driving traffic to online initiatives, and the brand-building effects of online activities;
- business—to translate business needs to measurement requirements; and
- technology—to define data collection, aggregation, processing, and storage strategies.

Sound analytical skills represent the essential ingredient for web measurement. For larger implementations, a web-analysis *team* might be needed. It can be formed from people within the business, from an existing group of analysts, or from external recruits.

If a person within the organisation has the skill mix described above, this person is obviously the preferred web analyst because he or she already has a deep understanding of the business, and will ensure that data are analysed within an appropriate business context.

Web analysts should be fluent with analytical tools and experienced in using a variety of analytical techniques—ranging from simple data aggregation, through statistical analysis, to complex data-mining. They should be able to distil the relevant information and able to produce sound recommendations based on exceptional business understanding.

ROLES AND RESPONSIBILITIES

The roles and responsibilities of a web analyst are many and varied, but can be summarised under the following headings.

Educating business users

The web analyst is responsible for *educating business users* about web metrics and the applications of various metrics in different contexts.

Identifying appropriate framework

The web analyst should *identify the appropriate framework* for measurement and analysis for any given business operation.

Identifying appropriate business owners

The web analyst is responsible for *identifying the appropriate business owners* for each area of the analysis, possibly in conjunction with business management.

Ensuring appropriate metrics

The web analyst ensures that *appropriate web metrics* are set for every aspect of the measurement framework. This should be carried out in conjunction with the relevant business owner identified above. For example, the manager in charge of the dealership network might be the owner of metrics concerning conversions that occur when a user locates a dealer on the website.

Selecting tools and services

The web analyst is responsible for *selecting tools and services* to be used in web measurement.

Developing new metrics

The web analyst *develops new metrics* or redefines existing metrics as they expire (or as functionalities alter). Different circumstances can cause the metrics to expire. These include a change of business focus, or enhancements or omissions in functionality.

Choosing appropriate analytical techniques

The web analyst is responsible for *choosing appropriate analytical techniques*, and for performing the analysis. In many cases the choice of metric will dictate the analytical technique to be used. If this is not the case, or if further drill-down is needed, an explicit selection must be made.

Communicating the results

The web analyst should *communicate the results* to relevant departments, stakeholders, and business owners in a timely fashion, and perform more detailed analysis (such as multi-dimensional analysis and navigation path analysis) as required, to further explain the metrics. This includes identifying action items to improve metric results.

Defining new initiatives
The web analyst is responsible for taking an active role in *defining new online initiatives* such that their contribution to the organisation's overall online channel is more predictable.

KEY RELATIONSHIPS
Web analysts need to have close working relationships with both business professionals and information technology (IT) professionals.

Relationship with business professionals
Much of the work conducted by web analysts is driven by the *requirements of the business areas* of the organisation. The web analyst provides business professionals—typically owners of various aspects of the online initiative—with data and analysis results relevant to their particular areas of interest or responsibility.

In turn, the business professional works with the web analyst in:

■ interpreting the results and creating decision alternatives;
■ tying analysis results to the corporate objectives to ensure that decisions support the organisation's business requirements; and
■ initiating process changes based on changes in the website, to follow up on triggers from the online initiatives.

Relationship with IT professionals
The *technology department* should assist web analysts to collect, cleanse, and integrate the data. The web analyst should provide detailed requirements to the IT department, including such information as the data needed for the analysis, the frequency with which these data are required, and cleansing rules and tools to be used.

In turn IT professionals will work with the web analysts in:

■ identifying the data requirements for metrics and analysis, and determining the data-collection techniques;

- advising on the efficient storage of the measurement data, and integration of these data with other data sources; and
- automating, if appropriate and possible, the capture of the data, and the consolidation and programmed cleansing of the data (but note that if data-cleansing is a manual process it is likely that the web analyst will take on this task personally).

ORGANISATION OF WEB ANALYSTS

In the early stages of web measurement, organisations might choose to treat it as a project, and not immediately create a dedicated departmental unit for this function. As the project team gains experience, as the practice stabilises, and as measurable value is delivered, organisations should consider creating a more permanent place in the organisation for web analysts.

Because web-measurement skills are extremely scarce, a business cannot afford to scatter these experts across the organisation. A web-measurement department enables web analysts and IT experts to work together to support business managers in their decision-making tasks. As the web becomes a more integral part of business, this department should not concentrate on web analysis alone, but can support all of the enterprise's analysis requirements.

Alternatively, if the organisation already has an existing analysis department, the organisation might simply upskill a portion of this existing team so these members can focus on web initiatives.

The organisation might also consider outsourcing these activities—in part or in whole. Despite the longer-term strategic advantage of bringing this competency in-house, outsourcing can be a sensible tactical option, especially for smaller organisations that do not have the money or resources to invest in these skills. Larger companies, however, *should* invest in the skills, because these can create a competitive intelligence.

REPORTING STRUCTURE

The best location for the web-analysis department varies from one organisation to another. The emphasis should be placed on how the organisation is using the online initiative and how strategic it is in reaching overall business objectives.

If it is placed too high in the organisational structure, the web-analysis department runs the risk of becoming disconnected from the rest of the organisation. If it is placed too low, it can lose its strategic importance. As an example of good strategic placement, an organisation with significant online marketing initiatives might place the web-analysis department at a similar level to the marketing department.

Gartner suggests that web-analysis departments should not be too large.[1]

> In an analytics-intense environment, such as a mid size financial institution, a typical Business Intelligence department might employ approximately 10 analysts; a large financial institution, about 30 . . . Managers of the Business Intelligence department should be analysts themselves. Services to the other departments should not be free because the added value to their operations is, potentially, enormous.

Gartner suggests that a subscription-based service works best, with business departments funding the web-analysis department and evaluating the results every year.

SUMMARY

Web measurement is a formal activity that should be conducted by a *web analyst*. The web analyst must be cognisant of the principles of communication and human psychology, as well as being adept with numbers. Web analysts should systematically monitor and analyse the performance of the website, and provide the information to business management for action.

The primary responsibilities of web analysts include defining a measurable, relevant, and balanced set of metrics, and measuring and analysing the metric results.

Business users should own the metrics and be responsible for their performances. Web analysts should work closely with the business users to define metrics, and then interpret metric and analysis results. The IT department should assist web analysts to collect, cleanse, and integrate the data.

Organisations might initially choose to set up web measurement as a pilot project. As the practice stabilises and delivers tangible value to the business, the pilot project can be moved to a more permanent place in the organisation.

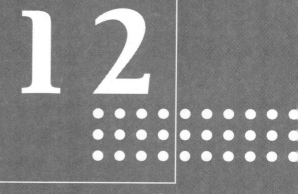

CHAPTER

12

Selecting Tools and Vendors

The market for web-measurement solutions and services is rapidly developing, but is still a long way from maturity. There are various commercial solutions available, and new ones are being developed every day. As the level of awareness of this subject increases, vendors are identifying potential growth in the market and are developing new solutions.

The basis of development in this market is no different from that in other sectors of the Internet technology market—learning and discovery. For example, the measurement of user activities through server log files was a discovery which created a vendor market segment offering tools to analyse these metric results. In turn, the issues of concern (such as overcounting from robot and spider requests, undercounting from extensive caching, and the need for extensive data-cleansing) that arose with the tools developed by these vendors created yet another vendor market segment which collected user-activity data at a *browser* level. This technique required insertion of a code into every page of a website, and this also led to a number of issues of concern—such as performance being compromised due to additional code, and difficulties in importing this technique to Internet devices. More recently, vendors have been looking at developing solutions that can capture user-activity data at *network* level. This technique has good prospects because it should address some of the issues that have arisen with the other two techniques, and because it is suitable for collecting data from Internet protocols other than HTTP.

As the focus of web measurement has shifted from basic counting of website traffic to the analysis of what really matters for the business, the scope of this measurement has expanded. Along with this, new vendors are entering the web-measurement solutions market, posing a direct challenge to more traditional players, diluting their share of the market, and forcing them to build rapid alliances and/or enhance their product suites. The new entrants include vendors who have been traditionally known for their solutions in other areas, but who have added web user-activity data, reporting, and analytical tools to their solutions. These vendors include:

∎ business intelligence, data-warehousing, and data-mining vendors aiming to offer comprehensive data analysis, integrating web user-activity data with enterprise-wide business-measurement activities;

■ customer-relations management and analysis vendors (such as campaign-management systems) aiming to integrate web-activity data with overall marketing and other sales channels data;

■ transaction-processing vendors (such as ERP vendors) aiming to link transactional data with web user-activity data; and

■ eBusiness platforms such as content-management and personalisation-server vendors aiming to integrate web user-activity data closely to produce more sophisticated content-consumption reports, and thus offer personalisation capabilities.

This has created an interesting market dynamic, with much uncertainty, placing web user-activity data at an intersection between these otherwise discrete vendor segments.

BEFORE THE SELECTION

Before committing to a particular web-measurement solution, organisations should certainly develop a framework and decide on their measurement priorities. This reduces the likelihood that the organisation commits to an inappropriate, often costly, solution.

The approach chosen to collect user-activity data will constrain the solution options, and will significantly influence the resource and infrastructure requirements. The preferred data-collection approach should be decided before the selection process.

The selection process will be constrained by the web-hosting service, particularly if webserver log files are the chosen data-collection point for user-activity data. Organisations that host their websites externally at Internet service providers (ISPs) might not have real-time access to these data. ISPs usually provide basic website-traffic analytical tools as part of their hosting service, and charge extra for the provision of webserver log files.

As discussed above, the vendors of many traditional solutions are now offering some level of web measurement as part of their service. It might be possible to leverage from the existing solutions infrastructure, and companies are therefore advised to investigate the measurement frameworks and priorities of these vendors. This might not only save companies from investing in a new solution, but also save them from unnecessarily introducing a new technology solution.

KEY SELECTION CRITERIA

There is a large array of solutions available—each with varying levels of capability and price tags attached. The range of possibilities in measurement also broadens the spread of the solutions that might be required for measurement. In the current landscape, it is very likely that organisations will need to procure solutions from multiple vendors, and then integrate them in-house. The measurement framework and priorities should guide the selection process. The key selection criteria, as with any other technology solution, should focus on seeking a match between the company's business requirements and the capabilities of the different solutions. The chosen solution is constrained by the costs of acquisition, integration, and operations.

For the technical aspects, the selection criteria should cover:

■ agreement on the definitions of standard measurement units;
■ data-collection techniques;
■ support for data-cleansing rules;
■ the ability to extract and integrate data; and
■ various other data-handling methodologies (such as aggregation and extrapolation).

Due to the relative immaturity of this market, and the relative inexperience of most participants in web measurement, companies should avoid overambitious investments in web-measurement solutions.

MEASUREMENT SOLUTIONS

References have been made to various technology solutions throughout this book. Some of these are tools that you can implement in-house as part of your technology infrastructure, and others are services that you should subscribe to for a time, or procure on an 'as-needed' basis. This section highlights these web-measurement solutions in a single table (Table 12.1, pages 212–213).

Table 12.1 Web-measurement solutions

Solution Category	Description
Internet traffic-measurement service providers	These services report on Internet traffic volumes and website rankings (overall and within-industry) based on metrics such as unique sessions, page visits, and visit durations. No one can measure the entire Internet traffic. Vendors utilise a variety of methodologies to collect, cleanse, aggregate, and extrapolate their base data to produce their results, resulting in discrepancies in their results.
Where from—to analysis service providers	These vendors provide periodic reports that show customer movements before and after visiting a website. Internet traffic-measurement service providers often offer this analysis as a separate service. The discussions on their methodologies apply to these services as well.
Online website-performance measurement services	These services periodically make requests from your webserver and measure server response-times. The operators of the site are alerted, usually via email, when the website is in error. The errors relate to connection and access to the webserver. Periodic performance reports are also provided, reporting various performance metrics (such as server response-times).
Usability-testing consultants and online usability service providers	Usability-testing services can be obtained from usability-testing consultants or online usability service providers. Online service providers use intelligent agents to perform task analysis. These simulate the behaviour of a web user as they see, think, and navigate through the website. They are programmed with a set of perceptual, cognitive, and motor characteristics to analyse a specific task

	within a site. In doing this they collect various time-and-effort measures of the visit.
	Classic usability-testing or focus groups can be used to verify the results of automated task analysis.
Server-based measurement vendors	These solutions capture the user-activity data at the webserver level, often webserver log files.
	Prices range from free to hundreds of thousands of dollars for licensing.
Browser-based measurement vendors	These solutions capture the user-activity data from the web browsers via a script program entered into webpages.
	Many of these vendors operate with an application service provider (ASP) model and charge periodically according to traffic volumes. Prices range from free to tens of thousands of dollars per month.
	There is relatively low customisation opportunity.
Network-based measurement vendors	These vendors focus on network-based measurement. User activity data are collected from the network by deciphering the content of data packets as they move across the network—also called 'packet sniffing'.
	Network measurement is best done at Internet service provider (ISP) level. ISPs have a 'bird's eye view' of all web user-activity data.
	In selecting vendors from this category, a close match between the demographics of the website and the vendor's arrangements with the ISPs should be sought.
	Network-based measurement allows measurement of user activities from other Internet protocols (such as chat, email, instant messaging, and file transfer).
	Subscription-based pricing applies.

For the *vendor names* and a brief review of each solution listed in Table 12.1, visit <www.hurolinan.com> [Locator Code 108].

MULTIPLE VERSIONS OF TRUTH

Reconciling the measurement results from different vendor tools and services is an impossible task, and has led to much speculation and discussion. There have been claims that certain measurement solutions can produce results twice as high as others, although objective evidence for this is lacking.

Such differing measurement results arise for several reasons, including variations in:

▌ definitions of measurement units;
▌ points at which data are collected;
▌ cleansing rules employed; and
▌ methodologies used.

Each of these is considered below.

Definitions of measurement units

Unfortunately, there are no widely accepted *definitions of measurement units* yet established. Vendors have different definitions for basic measurement units (such as unique sessions and page-views), which leads to discrepancies in the solutions. For example, one vendor might declare a unique session to have ended after 30 minutes of inactivity, whereas another might decide upon 15 minutes.

Data-collection points

As noted above, differences in *data-collection points* will also affect results. Web-server log files are not aware of caching that takes place at proxy servers and browsers, and therefore cannot record these user activities. Browser-based data collection, in contrast, is able to track these. As a result, the data collected from webserver log files are always different from that collected from browsers.

Cleansing rules employed

Regardless of the data-collection point, any user-activity data will contain non-qualifying data that should be *cleansed* before producing results. Non-qualifying data might include administrative and maintenance activities, and any non user-requested activities (such as machine requests, page-refreshes, and server-pushed pages). Whereas one vendor might consider certain data to be 'non-qualifying', another might include the same data—again leading to discrepancies.

Methodologies

External analysis reports representing overall Internet traffic are all based on certain data-collection, aggregation, and extrapolation *methodologies*. There are great differences from one vendor to another. Vendors who employ panel users might extrapolate the panel-usage data to estimate total Internet traffic volumes, and the traffic flows into particular websites, relying on some statistical justification of their panel size. This can misrepresent household and work usages, and probably will not include overseas traffic. Internet traffic-measurement services are discussed in detail in Chapter 4, page 86.

SUMMARY

The market for web-measurement solutions is rapidly developing, but is still a long way from maturity. The result is a large range of solution options from which organisations can select, with varying levels of capabilities and price tags attached to them. The choice of solution depends on your ambitions, and is duly constrained by your budget.

It is likely that organisations will need to procure solutions from multiple vendors, and then integrate them. Due to the relative immaturity of this market, and the relative lack of experience among practitioners in web measurement, it is best to avoid overambitious investments in web-measurement solutions.

Reconciling measurement results from different vendor tools and services is an impossible task. The discrepancies are caused by the differences in the definition of measurement units, the points at which data are collected, the cleansing rules employed, and the methodologies used.

CHAPTER

13

**Implementing
Measurement Practices**

Web measurement is an iterative, learning-based process. Organisations with no prior experience in the field are strongly recommended to treat initial web-measurement practices as projects. Figure 13.1 (below) provides a diagrammatic representation of the implementation approach.

The first phase is the *set-up*. This involves an assessment of the scope of the project, and various planning activities for its establishment. In the *pilot* phase, organisations should take a small and manageable aspect of the project and implement the measurement practice in this part only. During this phase, the project team should continuously refine the measurement practice. When it stabilises, you should consider a more formal place for it in the organisational structure. This is the *roll-out* phase. You will know that the measurement practice has stabilised when it starts identifying items for practical action from measurement and analysis, and when the business units have benefited from them. Once rolled-out, the practice becomes part of the organisation's business management.

Figure 13.1 Iterative implementation approach

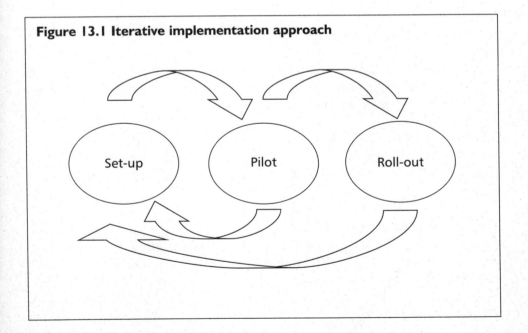

The implementation approach is iterative, because it involves taking a small and manageable aspect of the project at a time, and reiterating activities from previous phases where necessary. As the practice stabilises, organisations should move to the next phase in implementation. The availability of new knowledge and the desire to expand the scope of measurement might make it necessary to reiterate the activities in the previous phases. The reiterations are represented by reverse arrows in Figure 13.1 on page 217.

The rest of this chapter discusses the implementation phases.

SETTING-UP

The commitment of senior management is critical to the success of the project. Once the need for web measurement has been identified, a project sponsor with suitable decision-making authority must be enlisted to initiate and launch the project.

To commence the measurement practice as a project, the following activities are recommended.

Set objectives and define scope

Once senior management has bought into the idea, the internal stakeholders should be identified and brought together to define the *objectives and scope* of the project. It might be necessary to include external experts in these discussions, depending on the internal skills available.

A decision is then made as to whether to proceed. If so, there should be a clear consensus on how to do so. The project sponsor should lead this activity, communicating the outcomes to senior management to ensure their ongoing support.

Appoint the right team

Based on the objectives and scope of the initiative, a project manager and project team with the *right skill mix must be appointed*. The size of the team will depend on the scope of the proposed measurement activities. The skill requirements, and the roles and responsibilities of web analysts, are discussed in Chapter 11 (page 202).

Define the measurement framework

The project team should *define a framework* that is suitable for the business and for the audience group targeted. A generic framework is outlined in Chapter 2 (page 16). This can be customised in accordance with the specific business requirements of the organisation.

Choose metrics and analysis techniques

Within the context of the framework, the project team should define a balanced set of metrics in accordance with the objectives and scope of measurement already identified. Several considerations that affect the *choice of metrics and analytical techniques* are provided in Chapter 7 (page 135). Generic metrics and analytical techniques can be used to guide this activity, and are discussed for each layer of the framework in Chapters 4 to 6.

Identify data-collection points

Once the metrics have been defined, the project team must confirm that the required metrics can be measured, and that analytical techniques can be performed. The underlying data must be specified. The formula for calculating the metrics should also be specified and agreed at this stage. This activity will reveal *what data are readily available for measurement and what additional data need to be captured*. When data are not available, a method to capture these data should be specified. This might mean changes to functionality and design, or a redefinition of the metric. Chapter 8 (page 152) discusses data sources available for measurement.

Develop data-collection strategy

It is possible that the data required can be captured from several sources—each supplying varying degrees of accuracy and complexity. The most obvious example is user-activity data, which can be collected at three sources—the web-server, the browser, and the network. The project team must study these data sources and *decide on the one most suited to the organisation*.

In addition to the activity data, most implementations will require identification of the users who are interacting with the website. The project team should establish the requirement in this regard, and should select suitable user-identification methods.

In doing these tasks a special consideration should be given to the privacy aspects of the data being collected. Chapter 9 (page 158) discusses these three tasks.

Define data-cleansing rules

The *definition of data-cleansing rules* is an important step—identifying and removing the non-qualifying data from the measurement. Data-cleansing is essential to strip out data which might artificially increase the results. Chapter 10 (page 189) suggests several non-qualifying data types, and methods of identifying and cleansing them.

Define data-integration approach

For websites that *integrate with data processes* and other channels it might be necessary to obtain and integrate data from several sources before measuring metrics and performing analysis. Data-linkage points should be identified to facilitate integration. Quality of the data from other sources, and consistency of definitions, is essential for meaningful measurement. This activity should also specify frequency of integration and a suitable platform. Chapter 10 (page 193) provides a checklist to assist the project team in planning this activity.

Agree on basic measurement terms

There is no industry-wide standard available for *basic measurement units* (such as 'visit', 'page-view', 'user', and so on), although it is likely that some of the metric calculations will use these standard units of measure. To avoid misinterpretation, organisations should agree on the definitions of these units internally. These definitions will have an impact on the measurement results, and on the selection of tools and vendors. The project team can refer to Chapter 8 (page 150) for a discussion on the standard measurement terms.

Select tools and vendors

Once the scope and requirements have been finalised, the project team needs to *select suitable tools and vendors*. In-house implementation requires data collection and analytical tools. The data-collection strategy guides the decisions made at this point. Chapter 12 (page 209) contains a discussion on this subject.

PILOTING

The project team should select a pilot to demonstrate the benefits and achievability of the project. The pilot could be based on:

■ the agreed priorities of the metrics;
■ the ease of data collection; and
■ a representative sample of the metrics required.

Regardless of the approach taken for piloting, the scope should be small and manageable, and the objectives should be clearly defined. The outcomes should be measured against the original objectives, and a decision then made as to whether to proceed.

Once the measurement platform is established, the project team is ready to start the measurement process. Metric results should be produced and analysed, and a process should be initiated to communicate the results formally to the relevant business stakeholders. The project team must work actively with the business units to ensure the relevance of the results and to take necessary actions to rectify the measurement process.

The project team and the business stakeholders should jointly agree that the measurement delivers value.

ROLLING-OUT

When the pilot has been accepted, a more formal place for the measurement practice in the organisational structure should be considered. Acceptance of the pilot means that the measurement practice can identify items for practical action that will deliver benefits to the business unit.

For the operational system, the organisation should focus on creating a stable measurement environment. The end-users should be trained in interpreting the measurement results, and space should be reserved in the management agenda to discuss the results.

After a while, it might be appropriate to consider expanding the scope of measurement.

SUMMARY

Web measurement is an iterative, learning-based process. Instead of engaging in large measurement initiatives, organisations should define a relatively small aspect of the project for initial measurement. By doing this, organisations can enter into the learning stage as soon as possible and can expand on the initiatives that deliver real value to business.

This chapter provides an approach for implementing web-measurement practice in an iterative way.

CHAPTER

14

Predicting the Future

Web measurement is a new discipline. Although it is critical to the success of online initiatives, web measurement is yet to be fully embraced by organisations. Given its important and still developing role in the life of an online initiative, it is interesting to speculate how web measurement is likely to grow in future.

Here are ten predictions for the evolution of web-measurement practices:

1. The attitude of business managers will change. First, they will seek appropriate business cost/benefit analysis for their Internet investments. Second, they will demand the capability to track and analyse the performance of web initiatives. This is the only way they can assess whether these initiatives are working.

2. The Internet is here to stay, and measuring the success of online initiatives will reinforce its place in conducting business. As organisations take a more sensible approach to their Internet investments, and as they become more able to measure the value of these investments to their business, they will invest money and resources in this area with greater confidence.

3. Web measurement will move rapidly towards business measurement. This is natural because many organisations are starting to use the Internet for business transformation, and not merely as a marketing tool. This will require a close alignment and integration with the rest of the business and with existing business-measurement practices.

4. The vendor landscape will change. As the Internet is woven into the fabric of business life, measuring the success of online initiatives will merge rapidly with business-performance measurement. This is creating an interesting landscape for the vendors who are positioning to win this space. The winners will be those who provide flexible and measurable solutions that allow for modelling a measurement framework, defining metrics, extracting and integrating data from multiple sources, supporting various analytical techniques, and helping to produce outcomes for future practical action.

5. User-activity data will remain central to web measurement. Among the three distinct locations for capturing these data (server, browser, and network), there will be no clear winner. But network-based measurement will develop further, diluting the market share of vendors who focus on only server-based or browser-based data collection.

6. Most organisations will seek ways to integrate user-activity data with other data sources to produce meaningful metric results and to perform detailed analysis. There will be significant emphasis on vendors who can integrate user-activity data with other data sources.

7. Measurement activities will encompass other Internet protocols as they become more widely used. For example, Europe has already embraced mobile Internet access ahead of everybody else, and this initiative is likely to spread to the rest of the world soon. As a result, organisations will seek a common approach to performing the measurement of all online initiatives.

8. The privacy issues associated with personal data collection will continue to be debated. As organisations become more eager to understand their customers, existing privacy legislation will prove inadequate. Despite this, organisations will closely monitor changing legislative requirements and will comply with them. This, in turn, will increase the cost of data collection.

9. We will meet people who have the words 'web analyst' on their business cards. Web measurement will be a formal task and, although it will converge with business measurement, its unique aspects will always provide a role for specialists. These people will ensure that the online initiatives of an organisation contribute to its overall business.

10. This book is not definitive, and there will be extensive writing on this topic in future.

You can visit the accompanying website to stay abreast of future discussions at <www.hurolinan.com>.

REFERENCES AND NOTES

Chapter 2 Defining a Framework
1. Meta Group's research was conducted in March 2000, and published in *Information Week*, 1 May 2000.

Chapter 3 Applying the Framework
1. Meta Group's report on J.C. Penney's 'three-tail strategy' was published in an article entitled 'Charge up E-Commerce Synergies', by Jonathan Poe, June 2001.
2. Lindstrom, Martin, *Clicks, Bricks & Brands: The Marriage of Online and Offline Business*, p. 165, Hardie Grant Books 2001.
3. Simmons Market Research Bureau, August 2000.
4. The information in this case study is courtesy of Bruce Belsham, executive producer of ABC Television's *Four Corners*.

Chapter 4 Engaging Customers
1. Jupiter Research Centre, Online Influencing Off-line: The Multichannel Mandate, June 2000.
2. McKinsey & Co. study published in the *Industry Standard* in an article titled 'Thank You, Please Come Again', by Mark A. Mowrey, 20 March 2000.
3. Intertrust study, August 2000.
4. Nash, Edward, *Database Marketing: The Ultimate Tool*, McGraw-Hill, 1993.
5. Internet Advertising Bureau (IAB) Market Poll of 1000 online consumer adults 18+ was conducted in December 2000/January 2001 using Insight Express' banner intercept methodology.

Chapter 5 Explaining Dropouts
1. Andersen Consulting, quoted in article by Alexis D. Gutzman, 'The Truth Behind Shopping Cart Abandonment Rates', *Insights—EC Tech Advisor*, 29 August 2000.
2. Forrester Research quoted in article by Gutzman (see note 1 above).
3. Jupiter Communications quoted in article by Gutzman (see note 1 above).
4. eMarketer quoted in article by Gutzman (see note 1 above).
5. NetEffect quoted in article by Gutzman (see note 1 above).
6. Greenfield Online quoted in article by Gutzman (see note 1 above).

7.   Jupiter Media Metrix, *Retail Infrastructure Research*, 10 May 2001.

8.   McKinsey Quarterly, *The Duel for the Door Step*, 2000 Number 2, pp 32–41.

9.   Jupiter Media Metrix, , *Retail Infrastructure Research*, 10 May 2001.

Chapter 6 Containing Dropouts

1.   Forrester Research's Media Field Study published in *Webreference Update Newsletter* on 19 January 1999, <http://www.webreference.com/new/990125.html#survey>.

2.   Nielson, Jakob 2000, *Designing Web Usability*, New Riders Publication.

3.   The McKinsey Quarterly, *Segmenting the E-Market*, 2000 Number 4, pp 1–4.

4.   Jupiter Research Center, *Last Mile Strategies: Broadband Access Will Fail to Pave the Information Driveway*, August 1998.

5.   The Forrester Report, *Must Search Stink?* March 2000 by Paul R. Hagen with Harley Manning and Yolanda Paul.

6.   The Forrester Report, *Must Search Stink?* March 2000 by Paul R. Hagen with Harley Manning and Yolanda Paul.

Chapter 7 Choosing Metrics and Analytical Techniques

1.   The information is courtesy of Abigail E. Thomas, new media research manager, Australian Broadcasting Corporation.

Chapter 9 Collecting the Data

1.   Jupiter Research Center, *Last Mile Strategies: Broadband Access Will Fail to Pave the Information Driveway*, August 1998.

2.   Both CERN (European Laboratory for Particle Physics) and NCSA (National Center for Supercomputing Applications) are known for their pioneering work in developing the World Wide Web component of the Internet.

3.   See the Interactive Advertising Bureau at www.iab.net.

Chapter 11 Resourcing Web Measurement

1.   F. Buytendijk, A. Van Dorst, *Brains, Not Technology, Drive Web Analytics*, Gartner Research Note TG–13–3813, 24 April 2001.

INDEX